Reprints of Economic Classics

THE WORKMAN AND THE FRANCHISE
CHAPTERS FROM ENGLISH HISTORY ON THE
REPRESENTATION AND EDUCATION
OF THE PEOPLE

THE WORKMAN AND THE FRANCHISE

CHAPTERS FROM ENGLISH HISTORY ON THE

REPRESENTATION AND EDUCATION

OF THE PEOPLE

BY

FREDERICK D. MAURICE

[1866]

REPRINTS OF ECONOMIC CLASSICS

A<small>UGUSTUS</small> M. K<small>ELLEY</small> · P<small>UBLISHERS</small>
NEW YORK 1970

First Edition 1866
(London Alexander Strahan Publisher,
148 Strand, 1866)

Reprinted 1970 by
AUGUSTUS M. KELLEY · PUBLISHERS
New York   New York   10001

SBN 678 00592 3
LCN 68 18601

PRINTED IN THE UNITED STATES OF AMERICA
by SENTRY PRESS, NEW YORK, N. Y. 10019

THE REPRESENTATION AND EDUCATION

OF THE PEOPLE

THE WORKMAN AND THE FRANCHISE

CHAPTERS FROM ENGLISH HISTORY ON

THE REPRESENTATION AND EDUCATION OF THE PEOPLE

BY

FREDERICK DENISON MAURICE, M.A.

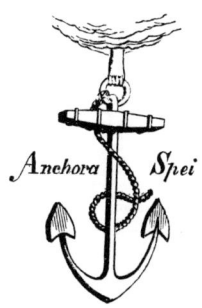

ALEXANDER STRAHAN, PUBLISHER
LONDON AND NEW YORK
1866

TO

Mr. J. R.,

FORMERLY A PUPIL IN THE WORKING MEN'S COLLEGE, NOW A TRADESMAN IN NEW YORK.

My dear R——

You wrote me an affecting letter last April, when you had just received the news of President Lincoln's assassination. I have often thought of that letter whilst I have been composing this book. It suggested the connection between the questions which are agitating your old and your adopted country. It showed how much you were imbued with the spirit of an English citizen, and, therefore, how solemnly, and with what brotherly interest you entered into the struggles and sorrows of the American people. You spoke warmly and affectionately of the studies which you had pursued, and of the friendships which you had formed, whilst you were with us. Perhaps these chapters from our own history will recall them to your mind, and will link the wonderful events of this day, in both continents, to the education which God has given our common fathers.—Believe me, very truly yours,

F. D. MAURICE.

PREFACE.

HOW I have been led to think on the subject of "the Workman and the Franchise," and why I have ventured to speak on it, I will endeavour to explain.

For eleven years I have been connected with a College, professedly for the education of working men. It started from the principle, that no education could be good for them which did not recognise them as English citizens, and did not aim directly at the object of qualifying them to perform their duties as English citizens. It assumed, that if we would benefit them as a class, we must first of all treat them as men whose highest interests must be the same with those of the millionaire or the noble.

Intercourse with even a small body of Englishmen who accept these as the principles of their union, must often suggest questions concerning the franchise; how any of us have become possessed of it; what kind of benefit we derive from it; whether it is valuable to us as individuals, or as members of a class; what amount of desire there is for it in those who are without it; whether they wish for it as individuals chiefly, or as members of a class; whether their exclusion is desirable or undesirable for the whole land.

It will be easily supposed that these questions must often assume a different aspect to us from that which they present to accomplished statesmen. Thus, for instance, the division of workmen into those who claim the franchise as a right, and those who will accept it as a privilege, may appear to us not quite an exhaustive one. We have known some who were impressed with the thought of certain *obligations*, from which no Englishman who has faculties for fulfilling them should plead exemption. We may even be conscious of having striven to cultivate that thought in them, rather than the other more complicated one, how they might wrest rights or privileges from those who have them in their keeping.

Again, it may seem doubtful to us whether the demand which we encounter for an expression of the real manhood of the working class in the House of Commons can be met merely by a vast expansion of the number of separate voters; whether we do not need some careful inquiry where the strength of this class lies; how it is most likely to make its voice heard, supposing its voice ought to be heard. On the other hand, if we are tempted by our own special enterprise to assume that the true force of the workmen must depend upon their education, we are continually reminded by our ambitious efforts and great failures how little any formal teaching would benefit our most intelligent pupils, if they had not the education of rough toil, of domestic sympathies, of national institutions, such, *e. g.*, as the trial by jury. So that we may often doubt whether the exercise of the franchise, *provided the sense of its being a trust could once be awakened*, might not itself be a better discipline, morally and intellectually, for the English citizen than the knowledge, however desirable in itself, which some would demand as the condition precedent to his acquisition of it.

And to the great inquiry, how *may* the sense of its being a trust be best awakened, our experience may at least suggest this negative reply. If you would crush it in one set of men as much as another, in the existing town or county constituencies, in any who may be admitted to it hereafter, make money the standard of worth, the characteristic glory of the citizen. If you take that course, you will reduce at last the upper, the middle, the working class to such a level, that it will signify almost nothing which have or have not the franchise—all will abuse it to the ruin of themselves and of their country. Therefore, to counteract by all means a tendency which has led, and does lead, Englishmen to sell their votes, their freedom, their souls to the highest bidder; a tendency which is at work in every civilized community, and is the seed within it of barbarism and slavery; this should surely be the first aim of all who educate; to this all teaching of arithmetic, languages, physical science, should be subordinate. Unless the gentleman commoner in Christ Church, the mechanic in Great Ormond Street, is reminded that he has relations to the human beings about him—to those who have left the earth, to those who shall be on it when he has left it—which are stronger than all the accidents that separate one class from another, it is hard to say which will grow to be the more ignominious man, which will do least good or most mischief to the land.

These thoughts, however precious to ourselves, we might have kept to ourselves. A very secular motive led me to utter them. The rooms in our college became too small for the pupils who frequented it. We desired to build new rooms. Very reluctantly we determined that we must ask for help from the public. It seemed right, first, that we should try to earn some money before we begged for it; secondly, that we should show some excuse for our begging. It was suggested that a course of lectures might be delivered which should explain the objects of our college. But they can be explained very easily without such a course. A single sheet contains an account of our teaching. Any one can come and see what we are doing. General disquisitions would be wearisome and superfluous. A commendation of our own modes or our success would be more odious to the speaker than even to the hearers. If the lectures could turn on some topics connected with the state and capacities of the working class—which were at the time occupying the thoughts of the other classes —both these objections might perhaps be avoided. An impression had been left on the minds of many intelligent and well-disposed persons by the very able speech of Mr. Lowe against the bill of Mr. Baines, that any extension of the suffrage to workmen implied a concession to mob force, a concession which some said was a needful one, which Mr. Lowe, with more manliness, denounced as ignoble. A person who sincerely believed that a new life-blood would be poured into the body politic if the workmen had a stronger feeling that they were an integral portion of it, might endeavour to explain why he held this opinion. Suppose he could show that instead of reverencing mob force, he regarded the cry to be represented as a pledge that those who make it despise and repudiate mob force; that instead of being indifferent to the old maxims of the constitution he wished to recover them: a few persons of the middle and upper classes might be induced to reconsider the grounds of their fears, a few of the working class to set more distinctly before themselves the nature and object of their hopes. Lectures of this kind, linking together the education and representation of the people, would illustrate the purpose for which a college of working men might serve, better than any formal arguments or any egotistical apology for our own.

A series of such lectures on the representation of the people were read to a very small circle of ladies and gentlemen, who kindly consented, for the sake of the object, to come to a street in the north of London in the very midst of the London season, and on the eve of the general election. The price of the tickets, though far too high for the value received in exchange, of course added very little to the funds of the College. The liberality of a publisher enabling me to make a considerably larger contribution to them induced me to print what I had written. I have adopted for the lectures the title of " Chapters from the History of England," which corresponds faithfully to their contents. They attempt to set forth the growth of our people in successive periods. I have wished especially to trace the influence of the culture and belief of the nation, under our different dynasties, upon the House of Commons, and its reciprocal influence on them. The imperfections and errors of this experiment will, I trust, be imputed solely to me; any hints in it which may assist the reader in connecting the perplexities of other days with those of our own, and in seeing a path out of them, I would thankfully trace to the College, the pupils in which have taught me far more than they have learnt from me.

CONTENTS.

CHAPTER I.

How the Roman, Saxon, and Norman Times illustrate the Words People, Citizen, Representation, Education, Commons, Freeholder, Freeman 1

CHAPTER II.

The House of Commons from the Reign of Henry III. to the Reign of Henry VII. 33

CHAPTER III.

The House of Commons in the Tudor Period . . . 65

CHAPTER IV.

The House of Commons in the Stuart Period . . . 98

CHAPTER V.

The House of Commons in the Eighteenth Century . . 136

CHAPTER VI.

THE HOUSE OF COMMONS IN THE NINETEENTH CENTURY . . 168

CHAPTER VII.

MANHOOD SUFFRAGE AND MONEY SUFFRAGE 204

INDEX 241

REPRESENTATION AND EDUCATION.

CHAPTER I.

HOW THE ROMAN, SAXON AND NORMAN TIMES ILLUSTRATE THE WORDS PEOPLE, CITIZEN, REPRESENTATION, EDUCATION, COMMONS, FREEHOLDER, FREEMAN.

THE words, Representation of the People, Education of the People, are continually ringing in our ears. It is felt by all, that Education and Representation must be connected with each other. *How* they are connected, how one depends upon the other, is a question of deep interest to England.

I propose to consider this question. I desire not to treat it speculatively, but practically; not to propound certain theories of my own upon it, but to consider what light history—especially the history of our own country—throws upon it.

I have said the *words* People, Representation, Education, are ringing in our ears. There is a danger of these words passing into mere sounds. There is a danger of our affixing to them loose, capricious senses, or senses derived from particular times and accidents. Let us begin with examining them a little; not for the purpose of finding such definitions of them as might appear in a dictionary, but that we may have some impression of their living force, that we may use them intelligently. The word *People* we may perhaps give ourselves credit for understanding without any examination. I suspect that it is one about which we are specially liable to fall into mistakes. Even our best writers will not always help us to avoid mistakes, until we have reflected upon their language, and have profited by information which they may not have possessed.

Take an instance from Shakespeare's " Coriolanus." That play is founded on an old tradition preserved in the patrician families of Rome. Though it may have no positive historical foundation, it embodies most remarkably, most truly, the spirit of Roman history. It exhibits faithfully the temper of a class which was vindicating to itself the exclusive right to the government of the commonwealth, to the privilege of citizenship. That class is represented by an individual man of distinct purpose, great courage, within his own circle of warm affections, full of contempt for all who lie outside of that circle. Shakespeare has thoroughly appreciated the force of the story in this sense. No one could have made us feel it as he has done. We have accepted the play as a substantive part of our literature. It is truly English, as well as truly Roman. It assists us in understanding our own men, as well as the men of the old world,—the good and evil of the patricians who have been born on our soil, as well as of those who belonged to the mistress of the world.

If you turn to the first scene of this great drama, you will find a Roman citizen saying, " You know Caius Martius is chief enemy of the *people.*" And another speaks of Menenius Agrippa, as " one that always loved the *people.*" It would be worse than hypercriticism to complain of Shakspeare for using the word " people " here. It would be sheer ignorance. It would be demanding from him a knowledge of Roman habits which we ought to be aware that he could not have. And it would be to lose the benefit of the knowledge which he had of modern habits—a knowledge which unconsciously modified and determined his expressions about other times. But it is right for us to understand that he was using the word people in exactly the opposite sense to that in which Caius Martius, or Menenius, or any Roman patrician of any age, would have used it. Instead of despising the people, or favouring the people, they would have said, " We, the members of the old families, *are* the people ; you plebeians have no pretension to that great and honourable name."

If you turn from Shakespeare's plays to the " Lays of Ancient Rome," by Lord Macaulay, you will meet with a very inferior exhibition of the internal, the great moral struggle between the patrician and plebeian spirit in Rome. But you will see that the later writer, possessing all the modern erudition upon the subject of Roman history—saturated also with the thoughts and conceptions of his own history—is able to find exactly the right substitute for the expression of our dramatist. Where Shakspeare uses the word *people,* Lord Macaulay uses the word *commons.* No better, no more instructive translation of the Latin *plebes* could be found. It throws back a light upon the annals of the great Italian state. It removes many confused impressions from the annals of our English state; especially, I would add, from the annals of our representation. I hope to show you presently what I mean. But I have a little more to say first about the relations of the old Roman people to the men who aspired to be sharers of their position, who claimed to be recognised as really—not merely by the accident of neighbourhood—fellow-citizens.

The patricians were undoubtedly possessors of lands. Many of the questions between them and the plebeians turned upon the possession of lands, especially of those which were acquired by conquest. But land was the sign of the ancient family. It had permanence. It could be transmitted from father to son. It was the witness of the endurance of the race. If, therefore, rights to land were one topic of contention between those who wished to keep the name of people to themselves, and those who demanded a share in that name, questions about marriage, ultimately about the intermarriage of plebeians with patricians—questions, that is to say, concerning the family principle itself—formed a still more vital subject for controversy. Another subject of debate related to the claims which the owners of property had upon the persons of those who had come under obligations to them. That power over the person reduced the debtor, probably, into very much the condition of the slave who had been the prize of conquest. The distinction between the two cases seemed to be almost in favour of the last. And yet could one who claimed to be a Roman bear that the difference between them should be effaced?

Here, then, we have come to *the* characteristic which the patrician boasted of as his own, which the plebeian was more and more determined to assert as his also. The patrician was the *Free Man*. He was also the freeholder. He had land by transmission and inheritance. That was the token of his dignity, of his lordship. The word "free" might often seem to him inseparable from this possession. But he knew—he confessed, in a thousand ways—that it had another and deeper signification. If he had not a hide of land, still it behoved a Roman to be a free man. At all hazards, at all sacrifices, he must maintain his freedom.

Caius Martius Coriolanus embodies distinctly, to our imagination, the sense of freedom as it dwelt in the heart of the Roman patrician. The opposition to him makes us feel how the same sense was awakened in the heart of the plebeian. And we perceive also, partly in this story, more clearly in all the actual records of Roman life, what school nurtured this sense, both in one and in the other; where both learnt entirely to separate the idea of freedom from the idea of savage independence; to regard the last with contempt, in proportion as they prized the first. The camp was the real education of the Roman,—of the lordly race and the aspiring race. There was brought out the consciousness of a country which both were to defend, in which both were interested. There the general came to perceive that his authority was a service, that he could only be above his soldiers if he encountered their risks, or greater risks than theirs, if he shared their privations. There the soldiers learnt the sacredness of law, the necessity and the blessing of obedience. The oath of service became, indeed, a bond between them. As each man obeyed the word of command, as he kept his place in the ranks, he had a consciousness that he was one of a body; he rose by that very consciousness to a feeling of individual dignity, of self-restrained strength, which nothing else could give him. His religion, too, was the conviction of an unseen power which was knitting the host together, which was giving it a common united heart. Such a conviction expressed itself in acts, not words. But it moulded the society in the city as much as in the camp. There were conflicts in the first which there were not in the second—conflicts of Orders, which there worked together against the enemy. But the conflicts were all pointing towards some reconciliation of forces; each Order, in its very effort to be exclusive, was discovering that it could not exist without the other. The conflicts, like the battles abroad, became part of the Roman education. Out of them was formed the City, which was to exercise so mighty an influence over the destinies of all cities in the time to come. The grand principles were asserted in Rome amidst all its contradiction, that a people can only consist of freemen; that the freeman and the citizen are interchangeable names; that freedom cannot be attained till all are under the dominion of the same law; that law becomes itself an oppression if there is not a living sympathy between those who obey it and those who administer it; that freedom and citizenship are impossible where discipline is wanting; that discipline loses its name, and becomes the management of a machine, if it does not aim at forming citizens and freemen. After-ages were to develop these great maxims; to remove monstrous contradictions from their application; to elevate the idea both of freedom and education; to expand the conception of a people; to connect the citizen much more closely with the man. But the maxims were never to become obsolete. The records of every country of the modern world were to enforce and illustrate them—no records more than those of our own land.

I have given a hint or two about the words people and education, which may become more intelligible hereafter. But can we learn anything about the word representation from the Roman story?

There is a passage in "Coriolanus" which states, as well as any prose narrative could, a great fact in Roman history, a fact that marks a crisis in it, and which, at the same time, reveals most strikingly the temper of the Roman aristocrat, and the light in which he regarded, not the people, but the commons. Caius Martius is talking with his more moderate and reasonable friend, Menenius Agrippa, about some concessions which had been made to the plebeians by the Senate, concessions which, of course, seem to him cowardly and ignominious. Menenius asks—

> What is granted them?
>
> *Mar.* Five tribunes to defend their vulgar wisdoms,
> Of their own choice: one's Junius Brutus,
> Sicinius Velutus, and I know not.—'Sdeath!
> The rabble should have first unroof'd the city,
> Ere so prevail'd with me: it will in time
> Win upon power, and throw forth greater themes
> For insurrection's arguing.
>
> *Men.* This is strange.
>
> *Mar.* Go, get you home, you *fragments!*

That word *fragments* is chosen with marvellous skill. It expresses better than any epithet could the scorn of Martius for a mere crowd. It has nothing organic in it; nothing of the fellowship which belongs to a race; nothing of the cohesion which is in an army. He despises those who form the crowd for this reason. And if the assumption were a true one, if these plebeians had been only fragments, one would recognise in the scorn the sentiment of a gallant soldier who entered Corioli alone, who felt in himself how much manhood is above multitude. But Caius Martius was uttering a falsehood—a falsehood which has been odious in those who have repeated it in later days, if it was not so in him. These men were *not* fragments. They belonged to families. They had mothers, if not so stately as Volumnia; wives, if not so full of fears as Virgila. They had a past in their ancestors, as he had in his : a future in their children, as much as he could have in his. And they were members of the same city, whether he thought so or not. How could that be proved? How could it be shown that they were not fragments; that they were organic; that they had a common mind? It was shown by that demand for tribunes which the Senate, in spite of its own reluctance, in spite of the remonstrances of such men as Caius Martius, was forced to concede. When the plebeians elected tribunes, they refused to be treated as portions of a mass or a mob. They proved themselves an integral portion of the commonwealth. Now, any man who acts as the spokesman of a number of men, any one to whom they habitually commit the management of their interests, the defence of their privileges, is their *representative*. The tribunes of the plebeians were the representatives of the plebeians. From the time that these tribunes became one of the institutions of Rome, the plebeians were represented in the state. They might acquire a further representation afterwards ; they might become eligible for various functions in the state; they might make their voices heard through various organs. But whenever they did make their voices heard through any organs which they selected, and not merely by force of numbers, and the cries which numbers could raise, they were represented. The disgust which Caius Martius is supposed to have felt for this representation was a natural disgust in a patrician who wished his Order to be the people. But it was an unpatriotic disgust; it was ultimately a suicidal disgust. If the patrician reverenced organisation, despised what was inorganic, he should have desired that all the loose fragments which he saw moving about him should become organic. If he wished to assert Rome as a city of freemen, he should have welcomed the cry for freedom in all who dwelt under its shadow. That would have been the true security for the reverence of the old families.

That the Romans of the old families had but seldom this faith, that they thought the strength of the commonwealth dwelt in them, and that the adoption of any new forces into it must tend to its weakness, is grievously true. And it is also true that the sorest punishment awaited them for this want of wisdom and justice. The multitude which they would not raise to be a people, found leaders to flatter it and pamper it as a multitude; leaders from whom it would receive, not an education, but bread and entertainments to prevent it from seeking an education, to keep it lazy and brutal. These leaders of the mob, when they had made themselves its dictators, might allow them all the names which once denoted the existence of a people, which marked how their fathers had striven to be a people. What harm could the names do when all which they signified was departed? What harm could it do to throw about the title of citizenship with magnanimous profusion, when citizenship implied no fellowship in a body? What harm could it do to bestow an unlimited privilege of voting, if voting involved no representation? And the old families—why should not they retain all the images and household gods which told of ancestors who could govern, if the actual government had passed to mere officials; if the family feeling, with all the virtues which appertained to it, was utterly dried up; if all visions of the past, and hopes of the future, were buried in a dull and miserable present, given up to luxury and lies?

Here was that abyss which the Roman aristocracy saw opening before them, for which civil wars and proscriptions were preparing the way, which some of the most courageous of them thought they could avert by cutting off the man whom the soldiers and the people counted as their champion, and who actually did sympathise with them as none of the exclusive patricians had done. What could such a murder avail to arrest the establishment of a tyranny over hearts which had become slavish; which the lust of conquest, and the gold that was the fruit of conquest, were making more slavish because more venal; which was losing the sense of freedom and of law through that discipline that at first had done so much to awaken the sense of both; which was drawing disorder and death to itself from those very provinces to many of which it was imparting order and life? For this mighty encouragement, this blessed proof of a Divine government over the world, comes to us out of the contemplation of that empire which carried in it the seeds of its own inevitable decline, of its ultimate fall; that it was preparing the countries which it ruled for freedom and healthy government, and a noble civilization, whilst these were perishing within itself. Those countries might often groan under the yoke of governors who had imbibed the debasing maxims of the capital, and only went forth to eat up their fruits, to torment their inhabitants. But they also experienced the blessing of being guided by wise and honest men, who had inherited the traditions of Roman law and equity, who believed that the task of Rome was to conquer only that it might improve. Such men could not form a people, or give the provinces the education which a people requires, or teach them the meaning of representation. They could establish in the provinces institutions which had once denoted the existence of a people, which expressed the results of their education, which had represented their mind. Such institutions might last on till other influences came over the lands wherein they existed, which should convert them into instruments of education, which should cause them to embody the wishes and purposes of freemen.

I need not tell you that the grandest of these influences for the regeneration and reconstruction of society seems to me that proclamation of a kingdom utterly opposed in its principles and its object to the kingdom of the Cæsars, which proceeded from Judea just as that kingdom was supplanting the old Roman republic. In every way that proclamation encountered the imperial conception and the imperial practice. The gods of the empire upheld the despotism of a military ruler over all the different races which had confessed the might of the Roman arms. The God who spoke in the Gospel was emphatically the deliverer of men out of bondage; He could be described by no other name. The man who reigned by the power of arms was recognised as a god in virtue of his power. The Man who was set forth as the Head of all men by the Church, had proved His Godhead by stooping to the weakness of all His subjects, to the death of the cross. The Cæsars tolerated the different religions of the provinces on condition that each ministered to the supreme monarch. The message went into all nations that there was a Spirit of God calling them to be members of one body, but assigning to each offices and functions suitable to its own place and circumstances. This Spirit was especially announced as the Spirit of Liberty.

All the conditions of the new society stood in the same striking contrast to those of the empire into the midst of which it had come. There is an imposing sense of multitude, if one reckons up the subjects of the Cæsars, with all their different customs and dialects. Nothing is so striking as the insignificance of those bodies which rose up in the different provinces, each claiming to be a section of the Christian kingdom. The enumeration of the treasures which were accumulating as the centre of the world, and were pouring in from all parts of its circumference, is appalling. The poverty of these bodies is as conspicuous as their smallness. Yet they are distinctly organic—they have a strong sense of being connected as a family under an elder Brother, who is gone out of sight, and a divine Father. They claim to be a people, as the old families of Rome did. They believe themselves to be the subjects of an education by the Divine Spirit. Each of them is to help in the education of the rest. There are persons who represent the body of which they are members, who are recognised as its representatives by the other bodies which belong to the same fellowship. Many, therefore, of the ideas of the old republic seem as if they were starting again into life; that fundamental idea of freedom being inseparable from obedience, of the highest being servant to the lowest, finds here its justification, its full manifestation, its hidden root. There was, no doubt, this amazing difference between the Christian and the old republican conception, that the Man was exalted above the Roman, that the message was addressed to Jew, Greek, bond and free.

THE CLERGY AND THE PEOPLE. 15

But it was not a message which levelled the freeman to the condition of the slave. That was the effect of the imperial system. A dead equality was what it practically recognised, what it was always threatening to produce. The Gospel spoke of the slave as redeemed and raised to the highest privileges of the citizen.

Such an organisation as this could not be tolerated by an empire which felt its own existence to rest on very insecure foundations. The persecutions, on the whole, gave consistency to the body which they sought to extirpate. But the maxims of the empire affected that body in a multitude of ways most injuriously, even whilst they were open enemies. One distinction which particularly disturbed the use of the word "*People*" grew up in the midst of a persecution, was almost caused by it. The clergy were sharply divided from the laity or the body of the people. The ministers or servants claimed to be masters. The nomenclature was Greek, but the Church which most eagerly adopted it was Latin. It soon connected itself with all the habits of the Latin mind when the Church and the empire were reconciled. The clergy were accepted as a privileged order. Those who entered that order ceased to be a portion of the people. Had there been nothing to counteract this habit of feeling in the constitution of the Church itself—in its fundamental principle—and had the ecclesiastics been permitted to mould European society according to their conception—the result must have been a caste system, like that in Hindostan. But it was not to be so. If the Church was to be the instrument of imparting a new civilization, it was to work on materials already provided for it. To know what it could do, we must know what those materials were. Our England was to take its shape from an order which had been recognised by the worshippers of Odin, from institutions left for it by old Rome, before it was to receive any impression from the new Rome of Gregory and Augustine.

I suppose there are no conclusions about which Anglo-Saxon scholars are better agreed than that which one of the most learned of them has expressed in the following words:—" All that we learn of the original principles of settlements, prevalent either in England or on the continent of Europe among the nations of German blood, rests upon two foundations; first, the possession of land; second, the distinction of rank: and the public law of every Teutonic tribe, implies the dependence of one upon the other principle to a greater or less extent. Even as he who is not free can at first hold no land within the limits of the community, so is he who holds no land therein not fully free, whatever his personal rank or character may be." Mr. Kemble adds, " Thus far the Teutonic settler differs but little from the ancient Spartiote or the comrade of Romulus." " These," he says presently after, " are the first principles or rudiments of the English law, and in these it assimilates to the system which the German conquerors introduced into every state which they founded on the ruins of the Roman power." And then again, " However far we may pursue our researches into the early records of our forefathers, we cannot discover a period at which this organization was unknown." I must refer you to Mr. Kemble's interesting and valuable chapter on the Mark, in his book on the Saxons in England, for a full description of the most primitive form of society which he can trace among our ancestors. I can only afford space for two striking passages. The first relates to them before their coming to Britain. " I represent the Markmen to myself as great family unions, comprising householders of various degrees of wealth, rank, and authority; some in direct descent from their common ancestors, or from the hero of their particular tribe, others more distantly connected through the natural result of increasing population, which multiplies, indeed, the members of the tribe, but removes them at every step further from the original stock; some admitted into communion by marriage, others by adoption, but all recognising a brotherhood or kinsmanship; all standing as one unit together in respect of other similar communities; all governed by the same judges, and led by the same captains; all sharing in the same religious rites, and all known to themselves and to their neighbours by one general name." The other passage describes these same Markmen in Britain. " In general, we may admit the division of a conquered country, such as Britain was, to have been conducted upon settled principles derived from the actual position of the conquerors. As an army they had obtained possession, and as an army they distributed the booty which rewarded their valour. That they nevertheless continued to occupy the land as families or *cognationes* resulted from the method of their enrolment in the field itself, where each kindred was drawn up under an officer of its own lineage and appointment, and the several members of the family served together." Here, then, you have the groundwork of our English People—a society or organization closely connected with the land—a society or organization closely connected with the family. Yet, as Mr. Kemble shows us very clearly, not one which is the least like an Arab horde ; not a mere set of clans such as might be found among Celts; but a body of men, united under laws, and because united under laws, and because confessing obligations to each other, claiming the title of Freemen.

These Freemen had slaves ; if we attempt to conceal that fact, if we try to make out a better case for our ancestors than for Greeks or Romans—if we pretend even that these slaves lost their chains so soon as they heard the Christian message—we deceive ourselves entirely, we pervert and destroy history. Those whom they conquered did some of them—not all, by any means—fall into the condition of slaves ; we have no excuse for describing their circumstances as better than those of any other land in which men are considered the chattels of their masters. What we have a right to say—what we are bound to say— is, that the state of the freeman, not the state of the slave, determined the character of the society. Liberty was recognised as the proper condition of the Man. Those who claimed to be kinsmen—those who had common religious rites—were free. Whoever should hereafter be recognised as kinsmen, whosoever should hereafter be recognised as having common religious rites, must become free. The state of servitude was inconsistent with these. What a rise from the accursed equality of an imperial system, from the state in which the family was lost, in which the religious rites were only the signs and pledges of a common debasement, the protection against any attempts to emerge out of it!

The description which Mr. Kemble gives us is of a purely agricultural people; certainly not a *savage* people, for nothing can be savage which is organic, but wanting in all that civilization which is implied in the existence of towns or cities. In Britain this agricultural people found such towns or cities already existing. I know not where we can find a better account of them than in a book which I am sure is destined some day to take a high place in English historical literature, and which, I trust, will not be long left incomplete, though its excellent author has for a while banished himself to our antipodes. After pointing out the military origin of the Roman town, its type being, as we know, the camp, Mr. Pearson remarks:

"The nucleus of the town population consisted of Legionaries who obtained a settlement in return for their services. A motley array of traders and camp-followers grew up around these, while the old occupants were dispossessed by the new comers. To the last these colonists remained distinct from the British population, though every year must have added a British element to them. It is probable that for a long time the towns retained their military character. During this time they were no doubt towns in this sense, that they were not country; fortresses in the midst of an alien population; busy with the stir of trade; possessing the bath, the forum, sometimes even the amphitheatre; but centres of corporate, self-governing communities, they could not be in any sense. Before the end of the Roman dominion they had probably changed their character; the warlike habits of the colonists had given way to the arts of peace; the framework of civic institutions had been introduced, and the people left to govern themselves, perhaps by the very *laches* of the imperial government. But the liberty which they had at last received wanted time and peace to strike root; their municipal constitutions, their laws, their mercantile guilds, have all been transmitted to us, with more or less change, through the stormy Saxon times; but they were informed with a new spirit, and disguised under new names. The prefects, Scabini, and Curiales of our old cities were no more connected by popular apprehension with the mayor, aldermen, and common council of our own time, than Saxon architecture with its exemplars of Roman art. But, in fact, the constitution of our towns is as Roman as the bricks of St. Martin's Church in Canterbury." And again, in a very striking passage, in which Mr. Pearson confutes the common notion, that either the Celtic population or the Roman colonists were exterminated by the Saxons, he says, " If the Roman towns in some cases fell into decay, the poverty of a warstricken people and the decline of commerce and the arts of peace may well account for it. But the Roman colleges of trade were continued as guilds, Roman local names were preserved by the conquerors as they found them. Roman laws formed the basis of the Saxon family system, and of the laws of property. The Saxon conquest was a change of the highest moment no doubt; but it did not break up society : it only added a new element to what it found. The Saxon state was built upon the ruins of the past."*

These remarks are in strict harmony with those of Mr. Kemble, if we only consider *what* element the Saxon added to that which he found; how he availed himself of the ruins of the past. The new element was precisely that which the Empire had expelled. The Saxon restored life to the admirable institutions which Rome had set up in her colony; he made

* Pearson's " Early and Middle Ages," c. vi.

them institutions for freemen; he connected them again with the household; the family became once more the root of the state; the king was a king of men, not a master of slaves. His descent was traced to a mysterious ancestor, a divine leader of men who had shared in their toils, fought with their oppressors, won for them a settled habitation. The process by which these sons of Odin passed into Christian kings is worthy of all study. Augustine and his monks had certainly no thought of consolidating a nation. They would have brought England within the Latin world of which Gregory was the head; as the old conquerors had brought it within the Latin world of which Claudius or Severus was the head. The distinctness of the Saxon life they might gladly have abolished. But if this was in their wish, it was not in their power. The character of their own message hindered that result. It developed the sense of kingly power and kingly responsibility. It developed the reverence for women, for the sanctity of marriage. It developed the sense of freedom. The world's redemption could not be the most characteristic note in the gospel—addressed to a simple, practical people — without keeping alive and expanding all the associations which had clung to that sacred name. Old Roman ideas mingled with the preaching of the Roman missionaries; one of those ideas pointed to the emancipation of the slave as a possible blessing which did not interfere with the dignity or privilege of the citizen who conferred it. The distinction of clergy and laity was strongly asserted. All the dangers to which I alluded before lurked in it. But there was the compensation that the existence of the clergy bore witness that physical force, hereditary rank, the possession of land or of money were not entitled to the highest reverence. Wisdom was above these. The poorest man might receive a training in that wisdom—might become one of the clergy. This wit or wisdom must be the characteristic of the council, without which the kings could not decide or act. And if the wisdom of the clergy descended, as it so often did, into cunning; if the divinity of the office attracted, as it so often did, the laymen to desert their own duties for the cowl; if the clergy forgot their allegiance to the native monarch, in the sense of their corporate sanctity, and in the service of the Latin bishop; there was a redress, if not always an adequate one, for these evils. The spirit of the thane, if not of the king, rose against the ecclesiastical assumption, opposed the courage which is half-brutal to the intellectual cleverness which is half-devilish. Invasions of Pagan tribes, sweeping away churches, schools, monasteries, recalled the old Saxon strength which a perverted reverence for weakness had joined with ease and luxury to undermine. As Mr. Pearson remarks, the Danes saved England from becoming a part of the Carlovingian world. It is equally true that Alfred, fed in childhood with the national songs, cultivating the native speech, causing the most sacred and the most useful books to be translated into it from the learned tongues, did more than any one to save England from becoming a mere portion of the Latin world. He is to us the typical Saxon and Christian king; because we feel that he helped to educate a people, not a class; and that he restored to life those old institutions of the land which were grounded on the principle that wherever there is life, there must be, in one form or another, representation. The tithing, the hundred, the jurors, if we understand them aright, were precious instruments in English education, as precious as any books— making books intelligible. But they are also proofs that wherever a free community exists, it must have a mind or a soul, and that this mind or soul must have some other way of uttering itself than through noisy shouts. If we would reflect on that fact, we might arrive at a sounder idea of representation than we can get by connecting it with any single assembly; we may also apprehend what our house of Representatives has meant to our country in different stages of its existence.

All that has been told us of the Saxon people shows us that it has as much its root in families, and that it had as much tendency to become exclusive as the Roman people, from which we derive the word. The conquest of the Britons and Roman colonists gave the distinctions which existed in its order a new force and significance. The occupation of the land, of which an inferior race had been dispossessed, but from which it had not been driven out, made the honour of the freeholder—always, as Mr. Kemble assures us, greater than that of the noble by service —more intensely felt, the dependence of the unfree more vehemently and cruelly asserted. But that privilege of enfranchisement which lay in the original constitution of the masters may, by degrees, have been extended, almost unawares, to members of the subject race. There were also the humble kinds of enterprise which the towns presented to those who were less fit to draw the sword or plough the soil. Occupations necessary to the landlord and the warrior were pursued in them. These occupations became arts. They must be studied. They must be pursued in concert. Those who took part in them must have laws, must be under government. The wiser among them must exercise government. The members of the guilds, Roman in their form, Teutonic in the spirit, discovered that they were in the truest sense freemen. If the holder of land, subject only to the king and a common law, exhibits freedom under one aspect, the organization of trades exhibits it under another, and quite as real a one. The latter becomes more strictly and properly, though not exclusively, associated with the name of the citizen.

The regular clergy, though they frequently interfered with the authority of the sovereign, though their sacredness seemed to put a scorn on domestic life, nevertheless contributed much both to the knowledge of the arts in which the citizen was engaged, and to the form of his society. They set an example of an organized social existence. Their rules and obligations were imitated by the guilds. Cities were connected with the Episcopal see, with an ecclesiastical centre. The towns acquired a more laic character, and ultimately became homes for the secular priests. But at first, no doubt, their military origin, their commercial objects, were curiously blended with the lessons and discipline of the monasteries in their neighbourhood.

This Saxon life, it will be said, whatever was its worth, its weakness vanished before the Norman Conqueror. Not I believe the Saxon *life*. By the Norman conquest, as by the Roman, as by the Saxon, it was proved that nothing which lives can be swept away, that only which was *dead* finds the burial which it needs, and has been waiting for. The sottishness of the Saxon, the arrogance of the Saxon, the anarchy of the Saxon, the feebleness of the monarch who preferred to be an ecclesiastic, the ambition of the ecclesiastic who tried to be a monarch, the turbulence of the thane who would be a master and would not be a servant, these found their stern punisher. The will which could reduce all lands and all holders of lands under itself; the will which could apportion lands after its pleasure; the will which could lay waste lands for its entertainment—this was assuredly in the Norman. He was the king, and the foreign king. He might be the organizing king, such as the first William was, or the merely arbitrary king like Rufus, one who acknowledged no power but force, or the conciliatory king like Henry, who saw that force could not avail without wisdom. Whatever he was, he could create nothing, and, except for the moment, could destroy nothing. There was no doubt this great difference, which Mr. Kemble insists upon with much earnestness. The Saxon king was, he says, the king of men. The Norman king claimed to be proprietor of the land. I do not underrate the importance of that distinction. But I think the history shows that the Norman assumption served to unite the country as it had never been united before; that it gave the sovereign a power over the barons who held their lands of him, which his Saxon predecessors had never had over their thanes; that at the same time it enabled those barons to appeal to the obligations by which the king had bound himself to them; which obligations by their nature could not be limited to them, but must ultimately, if not at once, become checks upon their own violence; finally, that in this way the king was led to feel that the English were his subjects as well as the Normans, and that it might be his wisdom to enfranchise them in various ways, if it were only for the sake of curbing and counteracting those who were more dangerous to him.

And it must not be forgotten that the better part

of the Norman ecclesiastics did much more to further this assimilation than the Saxon ecclesiastics did to break down the barriers between classes in their society. They were more learned, they felt more the necessity of counteracting the pride of force which was trampling upon them. Anselm is not more celebrated for his philosophy or for his conflicts with William II., than for his solemn declaration when he came to Canterbury, that he should recognise no distinction between the races, that he must regard them as they stood in the sight of God, not according to the judgment of men. The instruction in the Norman schools, though it was purely Latin instruction, was not unfavourable to this equality. The sacred language was at least not the Conqueror's language. The English peasant might learn it as well as the Norman noble; probably he often availed himself of the privilege.

But there was another language than this, a language which had never died, a language which Alfred had vindicated for the highest uses, a language which, when it appeared to have sunk to the uses of the market, was really gathering strength and vitality to itself from its Latin and its Norman oppressors, which was in time to come forth clothed with their spoils, the organ of a glorious and enduring literature. Whose language was this? We must now revert to that word which Lord Macaulay, so felicitously I thought, used for the rendering of the Roman plebeian. The Norman *barons* or *lords* spoke the tongue which they had brought with them. The English tongue was the tongue of the COMMONS.

It is a word with which we are very familiar, and yet one which often confuses us. We are so used to talk of the *House* of Commons, that we do not always ask ourselves who inhabit the House, or how they came to need a House. If we did ask the question, history would give us a simple and direct answer. Knights of the shire, burgesses of the towns, these inhabit the House. Freeholders and freemen, these needed the House. There was a time when they did not need it; when they could not have made any use of it. But by some means or other the Saxon holders of lands have been getting quit of intermediate lords, have been acquiring the freedom of being merely subject to the king. By some means or other the Saxon inhabitants of the towns have been acquiring a recognition of their freedom, have been rising to municipal dignity. And now comes forth that great sign that these Commons have made themselves in very deed a part of the people. They have a language which is becoming rapidly the people's language. What the process of their education has been we may not always be able to trace. That it has been a stern one we know. Their schoolmasters have not been sparing of the rod. The events which seem most to occupy us in history have scarcely seemed to concern them. Had they anything to do with the struggles of the great Plantagenet king against the great Archbishop? What signified to them the victories of Richard in Palestine, or his captivity? Were their interests involved in the battle of John with the pope, or even in his battle with the barons? Yes; I apprehend every one of these transactions was affecting them in manifold ways, was conspiring with their homely life to prepare them for a change that was at hand. Grand principles were asserted, not on one side, but on both sides, in the conflicts of Henry with Becket. " The same law must be for all classes of my subjects," said the monarch. " But there is a law higher and more universal than the mere law of custom, than mere English tradition," said the prelate. The Commons had need that both those truths should be maintained, that some reconciliation should be sought for them. The lion-hearted king was not merely fighting battles abroad. He was leaving his subjects to all that fermentation at home which the romance of Ivanhoe, whatever be its mistakes as to the relations of the different portions of society, has set so vividly before us.

Think over that brilliant picture. Think what an utterly disorganized society it presents to you. There are all the elements which once went to make up a nation. The Norman baron, the abbot, the Templar remain. But all sense of law has departed from the baron, all religion from the abbot, all feeling of a lofty calling and connection with an order from the Templar. Will the discontented Saxon proprietor, or the Jester, or Gurth the serf, recompose society?

Will the hoards of the Jew be the instrument of doing it? Or Robin Hood and the foresters, who bear such clear testimony that the world is out of joint, and who fancy that they are born to set it right? There must be some fusing power which we do not discern in any of these; or the English people must fall into utter decay. Neither in the king, nor in the prince, do we discover any signs of such a power. In his "King John," Shakespeare perhaps gives us a hint, though drawn from another country, where it may be found. The citizens of Angiers, who bring the feudal monarchs to terms, may indicate what strength was hidden in the communes of France, in the commons of England, which might show itself hereafter, and might compel the acknowledgment of them as a substantive part of the nation, and prevent the whole from perishing.

But another work must be done before this could be done. The barons must discover that they are a living element of the nation, not an independent force which is crushing both king and commons. They must feel that the duty of maintaining the laws, of resolving that they shall not be violated, belongs especially to those who claim to represent a race, to sustain a history. If they perform that work faithfully, they may be allowed for the present to treat the commons as English churls—as beings of another creation from themselves. Their day will come. They will find charters established which they could not have won, principles recognised which can be confined to no class. The barons having asserted at Runnymede maxims which looked before and after, which were implied in the life of their own ancestors, as well as of the ancestors of the Saxon—which would be mighty for many more than their descendants—yet showed that something was needed to make them truly national. They could not trust their swords or their cause or the King of Kings; they must invite a foreign prince to defend their liberties by invading their soil. A Class was needed with sympathies less European, more tied to hearth and home, if England was to be saved. It might be ordained that a foreigner should vindicate the position of that class, should give it a representation. However the gift was obtained, the rise of a House of Commons would be the token that the freeholder and the freeman had learned the force of their names; that they were henceforth as integral portions of the people as the peers temporal or spiritual.

CHAPTER II.

THE HOUSE OF COMMONS, FROM THE REIGN OF HENRY III. TO THE REIGN OF HENRY VII.

IT has been the fashion of late to celebrate centenaries. With less violence than we often practise to make times and seasons fit, the six hundredth birthday of the House of Commons might have been kept this year. The writ by which Henry III. summoned knights of the shire and burgesses of the town to Parliament, bears date January 1265. That there were earlier instances of election by the freeholders of the counties may be true; it would appear that there is no previous recorded precedent for the coming together of both the orders.

There have been, I am aware, eminent antiquaries who have attached little significance to this event. In his "Merchant and Friar," Sir Francis Palgrave asks how it happens that the contemporary chroniclers take so little note of it, supposing it were a critical event in English history. There are two answers, it strikes me, to this question. One is supplied by Sir

Francis Palgrave himself in this very book. Marco Polo, his merchant, goes with Roger Bacon, his friar, to the shire oak. He discovers there "groups of peasants, who, it must be observed, [I quote his words,] were the representatives of their respective townships, the rural communes into which the whole nation was divided, and which had a species of chieftain, who, though it was evident that he belonged to the same rank of society, gave directions to the rest. Interspersed among the churls, though not confounded with them, were also very many well-clad persons, having an appearance of rustic respectability. These also were subjected to some kind of classification, being collected into sets of twelve men. These were the jurors, who answered for and represented their several hundreds." Now here is an organisation—a representative organisation—which must have been preserved in these county districts of England from the old Saxon times. If again we turn to Sir Francis's account of the London Guildhall—though the description is far less clear, being mixed with many allusions to passing controversies, which diminish its historical value—there are indications of a whole scheme of municipal organisation. A representation is found in the very heart of the old city, linked to its most venerable traditions. It need not have caused great wonder then, to contemporary onlookers, that this organisation should have received at any time a new development. Even if there were no more stirring events to distract their attention—even if all around had been peaceful—a particular incident which may seem to us of immense importance might have been overlooked by them. But, secondly, this was not a quiet time. It was the time of a revolution. All historians are impressed with the importance of that revolution; those who contemplated it close at hand were distracted and overwhelmed by it. As usual, the outside transactions in it, those which most affected the condition of the men who were passing through it, would be dwelt upon; some of its most pregnant acts, which have influenced generations to come, would be scarcely heeded. In 1265 the king was in durance. The writs which went forth in his name were really drawn by the Earl of Leicester.

That name is certainly not one which contemporary chroniclers have forgotten to commemorate. There was much to excite prejudice against Leicester at the moment. He was a foreigner; he had been the favourite, he was a brother-in-law of the king. He had become the champion of the barons. He had lost his reputation with them. He could be plausibly described —he has been often described—as one who only gratified his personal ambition, as a reckless rebel. He has hereditary claims to the suspicion of later writers. The worst atrocities of the Albigensian war were connected with his father. Yet he became dear to the commons. He was celebrated in English speech and song as their deliverer. He was the man, to borrow the title of one of Miss Martineau's books, who fitted the hour. The moment was come when a work was to be accomplished which had long been preparing. A House of Commons had become a necessity. He perceived the necessity, and was the instrument of bringing it into existence.

How this necessity had arisen, I partly endeavoured to indicate in my last chapter. I spoke especially of the English language as coming forth out of its swaddling-bands, as giving signs that it was not merely meant to be an organ of communication for those who bought and sold, but an organ of human thoughts, which should live from age to age. The Latin of the schools, the French of the law-courts, the more graceful language of the troubadours, must bow before it. The old speech of the Saxon strengthened and renovated, must be accepted as the speech of the Norman conqueror; even the monk of the cloister must use it habitually. Here was a revolution indeed; wrought out very slowly, unobserved by those who in different ways were taking part in it, but altogether irresistible, rich in its effects upon the institutions of the land, and upon every inhabitant of it, from the highest to the lowest.

But along with this English revolution there was going on a European revolution, apparently of the most opposite kind, likely to produce the most opposite results. In the latter days of John, and when Henry III. was a little boy, whose protectors were struggling in his name against the invading foreigner, the voice of the mendicant friars was beginning to be heard in every corner of Christendom, was penetrating into every hovel, and, at the same time, was compelling the professors in every university to change their system of teaching, or to give up their seats to the members of the new orders. *Orders* emphatically they were, bodies held together by a severe rule and by strong internal sympathies. But their power seemed to lie in their defiance of what had been esteemed the distinction of orders, in their indifference to ranks, classes, property, in the contempt which they poured upon the wealth of the high ecclesiastic as much as upon the family privileges of the baron. The Franciscans and Dominicans had different objects, their founders were of different nations, and of widely different characters. Their opposing tendencies soon became conspicuous in their followers; but they were alike in the qualities to which I have alluded. In the common sense, if not in the correct sense, of the word they were equally democratic.

How did this movement affect England? It must have a very powerful influence here as elsewhere. What the influence was we are in some degree able to guess from the story of a remarkable English bishop, one of the best men surely of his time. Grostête, afterwards Bishop of Lincoln, was completely carried away by the reports which he heard of the Franciscan preaching. He longed to be admitted into so holy and noble an order. The denunciations of ecclesiastical wealth, the honour put upon the poorest people, the implicit protest against baronial tyranny, were all most acceptable to him. An age of reformation had begun. What a privilege to have any part in it! Sir F. Palgrave's hero, Roger Bacon, was a dear friend of his. They had shared their thoughts and hopes at Oxford. They had worked at mathematics together. Roger Bacon had talked to him of mysteries in nature which it would be a wise and devout exercise to explore. What could he do better—so it is said, Grostête spoke to him—than take the vows of a Franciscan. Then he might cultivate with some hopefulness the life of a student; he would have the divinest sanction in his greatest experiments.

Thus dreamt the good man. Before many years had passed away, so Matthew Paris reports, two Franciscans came to Lincoln on goodly caparisoned horses. They were the agents of Innocent IV. for collecting tributes from the poorest clergy of the bishop's flock. The more he conversed with them, the more he began to think that they were upholders of a great European tyranny which must interfere with the life of the English citizen. It ended with his denouncing them as the servants of Antichrist, not withholding that terrible name from Innocent himself. He might have learned, had he lived a little longer, in what way the order regarded that student life and those devout experiments which were to have been carried on under its auspices; he would have known that Bacon was cast into prison as a magician by the superior of that very society.

These biographical passages would not concern us —they would be irrelevant episodes—if Grostête had not been intimate with another man who has not the scientific glory, who has not the magical reputation, of Bacon, but who is associated with the political life of England. "To the blessed Robert of Lincoln," says the chronicler who continued Matthew Paris, "did the Count of Leicester steadfastly adhere. Under his counsel he attempted arduous enterprises, ventured on uncertain paths, brought imperfect schemes to completion. For the remission of his sins, so it is said, the bishop bade him enter upon the cause for which he contended unto death. Some tell that the bishop once laid his hands on the firstborn son of the count, saying to him, 'My dear child, thou and thy father will die in one day by the same kind of death, struggling, however, for righteousness and truth.'"

From such a testimony we may gather how very sacred the cause in which Leicester was engaged appeared to the most earnest men of his age. We may also judge, and this is my main reason for quoting the passage, how much the Englishmen who were most likely to sympathise in the great European movement of the time, and had actually sympathised in it, were drawn in another direction—were induced to believe that a reformation, apparently of a far more purely national—what some would call, of a far more secular—kind than that which the Franciscans had inaugurated, would work more effectively for the great moral ends at which they were aiming. The words in which the chronicler I have quoted sums up his lamentation for Leicester, after his fall at Evesham, expressed, no doubt, the feeling of those who had the best education of the time. " Thus," he says, " did this magnificent man conclude his labours; a man who gave not only all he had, but his ownself, to relieve the oppression of the poor, and to defend justice and the right of the kingdom. For his knowledge of letters he was worthy of all honour; in the divine offices he was assiduous; he was frugal, faithful to his word, severe in countenance, constant in his prayers, reverent to his teachers; giving his nights to watching more than sleep."

Make what allowances you please for the partiality of this historian, he had the reasons which I have mentioned already for suspecting Leicester's motives; he must have had the dislike of a quiet ecclesiastic to revolutionary tumults; he had the reverence for the person of the king, who had been Leicester's captive, which an Englishman seldom loses. There must have been a strong conviction in him, and in numbers besides him, that Leicester had done something for England which none ever before him had done, and which could not be undone.

I have admitted, however, that if he was all which his admirers gave him credit for being, if he did all which we have ever imputed to him, he was only fulfilling that which must have come to pass by some agency or other in this period. No one doubts, I suppose, that the name of Parliament was an old and familiar name. No one could ever imagine that it was an English name, or that it was especially appropriate to English customs and usages. The idea of a king acting without counsellors, merely upon his own responsibility, is one which is as remote from Norman as from Saxon royalty. Independence is a barbarous notion for ruler or for subject, inconsistent with either name, only possible when both names have become practically extinct in an imperial system; when the monarch, instead of being really independent, is the victim of a hundred advisers, male or female, whom he may change from day to day; when the subject is independent in this sense, that he has lost the sense of relation to any master, of restraint from any law, and is merely the sport of all accidents. The feudalism which we impute to the Normans, so far as it involved a principle at all, was the renunciation of this independence on the part both of sovereign and subject. The freedom which we suppose to be latent in the Saxon institutions was equally incompatible with it, equally an acknowledgment of civic obligations, and of obligations due from one proprietor to another. The Saxon might speak of a council of the Wise; the Norman might speak chiefly of a council of the King, and when he cared to describe it, might take, as of course he would take, a word of French origin for the purpose; but a council could never be far from the thoughts of either.

Why, then, does the word *Parliament* thrust itself upon us in this reign of Henry III. with a force and emphasis which we never supposed to be in it before?

Why does it seem as if we had not fairly got hold of the word till we can connect it with the freeholders and freemen? It sounds strange to say so, but the assertion is, I think, abundantly confirmed by evidence, that neither the Norman king nor the Norman baron could realise their position to each other, could be what either was meant to be, till the Saxon element was combined with them, till each had, however reluctantly, done justice to that. I said in the last chapter that it is a great mistake to undervalue the strong will of the Norman kings, or to treat that will as a mere source of tyranny. How wild and weak it was when it became a mere self-will, the reign of Rufus shows us. How useful it was when it confessed an order, and sought to establish an order, we see in his father. How it sought an alliance with English sympathies, and gave a recognition to English rights, that it might not be crushed by its Norman subjects, we learn from the experience of his brother. What a tremendous anarchy was the result of this power being withdrawn or being divided, when the barons were left to assert the omnipotence of castles, the reign of Stephen demonstrates. It might seem as if the great talent of Henry II., and his determination to restore order, had abated this confusion. But then it was only to bring forth that other great struggle between the monarchical and the ecclesiastical power, to show that there was at all events one class which would not submit to be reckoned merely a part of the English nation. And when this question had seemed partially adjusted, we found in the following reign every indication that the most living forces which had been at work in the land, civil or ecclesiastical, were utterly unable to cohere, were exhausted, and had no secret of renovation in them.

I cannot take John's reign, as Lord Macaulay and some others have done, to be the commencement of English history. The barons, it seems to me, were true in their profession that they were only re-asserting principles which had been involved in all their relations to the king from the first. But in *this* sense it is the commencement of a history, that from his time each party confesses its obligations to the other. They are set down in letters; the record of them can be appealed to at all times. And then it begins to be understood that these relations can only be maintained either by force—and if by force, then it would seem from the invitation of the barons to Louis, by a foreign force—or else by a continual conference and consultation of the two parties with each other, not by occasional advices given by the barons to the king, but by a Parliament which should be an organic, habitual, necessary part of the State.

This necessity had worked itself out in the minds of the barons, as we see in the reign of Henry III. The Parliament was accepted as a legitimate institution, a part of the natural order of things, a return to the laws of England which the barons would not have changed. And yet there was in it the rawness, the incoherency of a new institution, which could not be easily got into a working condition, which involved perpetual collisions, contradictions, tumults, lying promises of the king to observe the charter, violent, often mad, devices of the barons to force him into keeping his word, or to punish him for the violation of it—a very hopeless, ineffectual conflict of acid and alkali which could never combine, till by some means or other that third element found its way into the mixture, till it was perceived that those Commons, those English churls, must speak somehow in the Parliament, if there was to be anything done in it, if it was not to be a mere battle-field between enemies who would soon have other battle-fields if they had that.

Now, I do not claim for the Earl of Leicester any special prescience, which enabled him to divine that, if the king summoned knights of the shire and the burgesses of the town to send their spokesmen to Parliament, he would provide what was wanting to this constitution, what might heal this disorder. I have no proof that any such thoughts occurred to him. He may not have devised the plan, or circumstances of which he knew nothing may have suggested it to him. It is foolish to speculate about motives, and imagine elaborate reasonings for any given action. The motives may have been better or worse than they look to us through the mist of six centuries. Reasonings justify an action when it is done, they seldom lead to the doing of it. But it would not seem to me strange that an enlightened foreigner, who had had many opportunities of observing the temper both of the king and the nobles, especially if he was intimate with the most intelligent and disinterested Englishmen, should have perceived more clearly than a native what might be needful for the reformation and pacification of the State. His popularity must have had some ground. The Commons would not have loved him as they did, if he had not given them a new position in the State, if he had not vindicated rights for them which they had never been able to vindicate for themselves. There is surely no improbability in such an opinion; though I care much more for the fact itself, than for any discussions about the author of it.

If we pass from the thirteenth century to the fourteenth, from the reign of Henry III. to that of Edward I., we may begin to suspect that all our conclusions on this subject have been mistaken; that the Commons really gained nothing by the revolution under Leicester; that it was a torment rather than a blessing to them, to have the right of choosing representatives either for burghs or counties. In that period the scene of the dialogue between the Merchant and the Friar, to which I alluded before, is laid. Sir Francis Palgrave brings Bacon and Marco Polo to the shire oak. The Sheriff is about to read King Edward's writ for calling a Parliament. His appearance causes the greatest dismay. An abbot, who is served with it, rides off at full speed to avoid attendance on his duty. The knight who is elected by the freeholders, chiefly by way of punishment, also flies, taking refuge in the sanctuary of the Chiltern Hundreds. The whole transaction appears to be utterly unwelcome to those who are engaged in it. We ask ourselves with wonder how the man could ever become a hero who inflicted such a curse upon those whom he pretended to benefit. Then we are transported to the Parliament House itself. There, indeed, we hear of petitions presented, and grievances considered and redressed. But it is the king who listens to the cries that go up from the sufferers. He has a body of Triers for examining and considering what help can be given in all cases of complaint. *He* has a claim to be popular. The representatives of the Commons seem to exist for the purpose of laying burdens on them. They are called together because taxes must be imposed—that is their special business—surely not one which is likely to buy them golden opinions of the class to which they belong.

All those statements I accept on the authority of so well-informed and excellent a judge. If he had not been composing a political pamphlet in the form of a mediæval romance—if he had been treating this part of our annals with the carefulness which he bestowed on the Norman age—he might have combined some other facts with them, and have presented them in a somewhat different perspective. But in themselves they are very valuable, and are such as we might easily credit from internal evidence, though they had not such learned corroboration.

Prince Edward, we know, spent the latter years of his father's reign in an expedition to Palestine. He must have had many things to ponder during his exile besides his chances of conquering the Mussulman—must have reflected on his father's blunders, on his deposition, on the course which it would behove him to take, that he might maintain something more of the dignity of a sovereign, and secure a class of more submissive subjects. A man he was, undoubtedly, of clear intellect, capable of profiting by misfortunes, with more kingly qualities than any of his predecessors since Henry II., perhaps since the Conqueror. If it was good for him to have the *prestige* of a knight in the Holy Land, he also deemed it good—so we are told—to spend a certain time at Bologna, the great University for Jurisprudence. There he would undoubtedly be complimented on his legal astuteness, and would receive many sagacious hints from admirers of the imperial code, as to the course which it behoved a monarch to pursue, in making it understood that the law issued from him, and that he was in no sense its servant; which hints Edward would duly and silently lay to heart, not without a suspicion that he could manage his own people better than any Italian professor could teach him to do it. He would have thought, no doubt, how inconvenient a set of legislators with local feelings and interests would be to him; how specially they would interfere with his purpose of establishing a general code for the whole land—of breaking down the customs and traditions of particular races. But when he found, on coming home, that the name of Leicester was still dear to the commons, that it was joined to songs, which might live as long as those in which French minstrels had celebrated the glories of Richard—he may have deemed it the more prudent course to accept his position, not to question the revolutionary origin of the new representation, rather to adopt it into his own system of government, only taking care that it should be as disagreeable as possible to those who had hailed it as a boon. From the monarch should come all grace, all redress of wrong-doings; the knights of the shire, the burgesses of the town, should be only thought of as a machine for extracting money for the use of the State from those who were most anxious to keep it for their own use. Such a policy would be in strict accordance with what we know of this monarch. Just as he tricked the Welsh into the acknowledgment of a prince of his blood—just as he taught the Scots to despise the native monarch, whom he had turned into a tributary—so he would cause the English to loathe the food for which they had craved, and to esteem simple subjection to his will much better than any freedom. And thus we should have a full explanation of the scenes under the shire oak and in the palace of Westminster, which Sir Francis Palgrave has so graphically depicted.

The policy was very ingenious. And like most ingenious policy, it proved abortive. The king was *not* found to be the source of all grace. It was *not* found that taxes were only laid on by the Parliament. He laid them on without consulting his barons or the citizens. Barons, ecclesiastics, citizens, rose against his exactions. Another rebellion threatened the land. That able monarch used the wit which was always at his command—used his strength —to maintain his prerogative, and to put down the resistance which became daily more organised. It was proposed that certain grave sentences should be added to the charter, of which this was the first:— " No tallage or aid shall henceforth be laid or levied by us or our heirs in this our realm without the goodwill and common consent of the archbishops, bishops, and other prelates—the earls, barons, knights, burgesses, and other freemen in our realm." A Parliament was summoned to discuss the proposition. It contained all the elements of a Parliament. But the king was in Flanders. He had not called it. The meeting of its members was as much a defiance of him as the meeting of the barons at Runnymede was a defiance of his grandfather. He consented to their demands. Of course, when he returned he withdrew his consent. The demands were renewed in a Parliament which he had summoned. There were concessions and evasions. The king asked the pope to cancel his oath. But the leek was at last fairly eaten. Dr. Lingard, I think, does not exaggerate when he says that we scarcely owe more to Stephen Langton and the barons who won the charter than to Archbishop Winchelsey, the Earl of Hereford, and the Earl of Norfolk, who were the instruments of establishing the sole right of Parliament to grant supplies for the king's necessities.

This privilege, it may be said, was won *for* the commons, not *by* them. The nobles and the prelates secured the addition to the charter, as well as its original clauses, though one as much as the other was for the good of the whole land. The objection is a sound one; if we had only the records of the reign of Edward I., there might be nothing to diminish the weight of it. Nay, if I looked at these events merely as establishing what is called "a parliamentary government," I might join with those who sneer at the importance which historians have attached to them. I do not undervalue the blessing of a real king such as Edward had the capacity of being, and such as he sometimes was; or the obstacle which a set of turbulent counsellors might often have been to the execution of wise plans. But it has been proved again and again that the false derivation of the name "*king,*" which connects it with can-ning or cunning, will be realised in fact; that craft, in the sense of mere power, or in the sense which it bears amongst us, will be his idol; that his life will become a very ignominious as well as very mischievous example to his land; if there is not some very distinct and emphatic voice which reminds him that a throne stands upon truth, not lies. Here was the blessing of those baronial checks upon the royal power which we have begun in our enlightenment to regard with a certain indifference or contempt. And there was a far greater blessing in reserve for the land. The barons, spiritual and temporal, were unconsciously labouring for a class which might prove the most effectual counteraction to their tyranny, which might support a really wise king in purposes that they were inclined to frustrate. Their assertion of the privileges of *Parliament*, if not yet regarded as an assertion of the privileges of the *Commons'* House of Parliament, would soon acquire that force. For there was a new strength in the Commons, which would speedily represent itself in the knights and burgesses who occupied their chamber.

To what causes may this new strength be traced? I have spoken of the Mendicant Friars, and of the immense power which they exerted in every country of Europe. That England was not an exception, the enthusiasm of Grostête for them is a sufficient proof; that there was something specially antagonistic to them in our English life, his case is also a proof. Nothing, doubtless, was more wanted in England than some testimony to the existence of a fellowship which was not bounded by its seas; nothing was more wanted than some testimony to its great lords and proprietors that the serfs on the soil, the slaves in the houses, were of the same flesh and blood with them, and had a portion in the highest blessings which they could claim. This testimony the friars bore: it was effectual, for it was true. But there was a negative side as well as a positive side in their teaching. They not only spoke *for* a universal society, they spoke *against* a national society. They not only honoured the poorest beggar, they dishonoured whatever elevates the citizen above the beggar. They scorned the order of the land as if it were something vulgar and secular; they levelled themselves to the most vulgar and secular habits of those among whom they went. Hence they provoked *some* indignation in those who were already an organised and conspicuous part of the commonwealth, an indignation qualified by the hope that they would help to make those who were not admitted into it content with their position. But they excited an ever-growing disgust in those who were aspiring to be a part of the commonwealth, who were already exercising some of the functions of citizens in their municipalities : and they excited a similar disgust in those who were trying to educate this class of their countrymen, to show them how they might fulfil their common duties better, and to give them higher aspirations. The English citizens, and the better part of the secular clergy, had equal reasons for suspecting and disliking the friars. Nor had they yet so far conquered the Universities that there was not a strong party capable of being stirred to activity, who looked upon them as intruders. Several of the colleges at Oxford were established chiefly to counteract their influence.

Now, the education of the commons of England in the reign of Edward I. is mainly due to the union of these influences. Wyckliffe is the man who is taken, and rightly taken, as the exponent of them. No one combined so remarkably the three characters of the university schoolman, the defender of the royal power against the papal, the secular priest or teacher of the commons. The three functions cannot be separated, though the first belonged especially to the opening of his career, the last to the close of it. All are connected with opposition to the Friars. The real work of his life—the translation of the Bible—would have been impossible for one who had not had the Latin discipline of a university and the English discipline of a provincial town; I may add, for one who had not acquired the Old-Testament feelings respecting the sacredness of a nation's life and history. In these feelings lay most of the power of the man. If the book did more than any teacher to keep them alive, it would not have been listened to or understood if they had not already been awakened in the English farmer and artisan.

But though Wyckliffe explains to us better perhaps than any one the process which was at work in our commons, it would be a mistake to separate him from a multitude of influences that were acting in the same direction. Unquestionably his translation struck the hour, just as Leicester struck it by his writ. And the writ would, I apprehend, have proved very ineffectual for its purpose without the translation. But the " Vision of Piers Ploughman on the Malvern Hills," had shown what the teachers of the commons were thinking about; how full they were of political and social grievances, how full of the sense of a political and social order; how these grievances and this sense of order blended with all their religion; what an unspeakable discontent they had conceived with much of what was passing under that name; how they clung to the conviction of a Divine government, which would in some way or other set the abuses of the world right. Our literature, our poetry especially, is born amidst these throes. And it is emphatically the literature, the poetry of the *commons*. You must allow me to be pedantical in the use of that word. It was not at present the literature of those who called themselves the *people*. The court had nothing to do with it. The baronial halls knew nothing of it. The higher ecclesiastics heard of it first to scorn it; then began to tremble at it. The pure schoolmen, those who had not, like Wyckliffe, come out into the air, could not conceive that it had any significance. Among the commons it had originated; they had listened to it with open ears; slowly it was giving shape to a number of strange impressions which they had received from the past, to others which were coming to them from the events of their own times.

That the wars of Edward III. compelled him to

have continual resort to parliaments; that in his reign the composition of the houses and their relations to each other began to be understood; that the practice at their meetings acquired a certain uniformity; that the knights and burgesses saw how needful it was to work together; that their complaints of grievances took the form of petitions, but that they denied the legality of any proclamation which was made without their assent; that their power, therefore, was growing steadily; that it was manifested in many of the beneficial statutes of the reign, especially in those respecting the papal "provisions;" these are admitted facts which few historians care to dispute. What I desire is, that we should associate them more directly and more closely than they have been associated, with that other class of equally notorious facts to which I have just adverted. The House might have been called together by the authority of the king or the suggestion of Leicester. It might have been in strict harmony with a previously existing agricultural or municipal constitution. It might have been sanctioned and made use of by the kings. It might have won privileges by the intervention of nobles resisting exactions on their order. Still it would have been a mere cipher; unless it had been turned into an engine of oppression, or an engine of rebellion. The nature and worth of the representation depended wholly and absolutely on that which was to be represented. If that was a dead thing, a mere fossil relic of Saxon times, to which an artificial momentary impulse had been given by a revolution, there might be all imaginable contrivances to make the representative assembly work; it might be constructed and reconstructed; it might acquire powers and lose them. It could mean nothing. But if the commons acquired a real moral life—if there were a soul in them—then all events would conspire to give that soul a true and effectual expression. Then the wars of Edward III., though undertaken to maintain his own title, would tend to bind together Norman and Saxon in the common English name; though never so purely chivalric and contemptuous of churls, he would give strength to the churls. Then let there be ever so many contrivances to make the representation a nullity—to make the king or the nobles the real electors—it would assert its own distinctness, it would do what they could not do, would speak what they could not speak, would prove itself essential to their existence, and to the existence of the whole land.

If the House of Commons had owed its strength to the wisdom of the monarch, or to his skill in devising a counter action to the power of the barons, its position in the reign of Richard II. would be inexplicable. Under the weakest of all rulers—that ruler who, according to Shakespeare's splendid irony—an irony true in spirit, if not in the letter—could talk of the divinity that doth hedge a king at the very moment when he was about to let the sceptre drop from his hand—there were parliaments which earned a better name from their own age, and did more for after ages than any which had preceded them; and the virtue of those parliaments certainly lay not in the higher, but in the lower House. For it represented those freeholders and freemen who had caught a new sense of their dignity and responsibility from the reforming teachers. The importance of those teachers as a political force is evident from the use which John of Gaunt sought to make of them. They may have been concerned—Chaucer appears certainly to have been concerned—in the insurrection of John of Northampton, which was a strictly civic insurrection, and was probably instigated by the Duke of Lancaster. It would be a great mistake, I apprehend, to connect them with the other more memorable insurrection of the same reign. If Wat Tyler did, as we are always taught, adopt those phrases and watchwords about the equality of men which became mighty in an after period—which had perhaps already been seized by the Jacquerie in France— he may far more easily have learnt them from the Mendicants than from their enemies. The citizen class would repudiate instead of hailing that language. Their religious teachers, in Richard's reign, still connected respect for the throne with opposition to the pope. Wat Tyler's movement is important as showing that there was a class which the House of Commons did not represent, which might some day become organised and demand to be represented in it; it is only an indistinct background in the picture of the age wherein it occurred.

But there are prominent figures in that picture which we ought not to overlook. The earliest literature of England, I have said, is the literature of the commons. It expresses the religious discontents and aspirations of the commons. Chaucer links their literature to that of the nobles and the court, and so becomes the poet of the English people. Contemplated from one side, he is under the patronage of John of Gaunt; he has a kind of laureateship; he writes legends of fair women. He is half French, but in an age when the French tale or the Latin tale, the French or the Latin song, must become English, even that nobles and dames may listen to it. And he can make it English, for he is essentially the English citizen. Therein lies his power. His melody is his *charm*; his love of fact, his sympathy with the forms and phases of ordinary English existence, his humorous appreciation of them, give all the *substance* to his poems. The man of the commons has not become the man of the court; he has only learnt just enough of its lore to make him capable of entering more thoroughly into the richness and beauty of homely life. He has been called a Wyckliffite. He is not that. He is simply an Englishman. He hates friars, because they are not English and not manly. He loves the poor parson, because he is English and manly. He and all his heroes and heroines are going to the shrine of the great English saint who had helped them when they were sick. It never occurs to him that there is anything superstitious in such a pilgrimage. He never thinks of asking whether Becket was a very dutiful subject of the king in his day, whether he preferred the monarch or the pope. These are merely antiquarian questions, or questions of formal divinity. Becket had acquired a national position, and a national sanctity; if friars, monks, and pardoners consented to pay him homage, that is accepted as a confession on their part that they have certain obligations to the country in which they dwell. The Prologue to the Canterbury Tales, the Tales themselves, belong strictly to the fourteenth century, to the century at the commencement of which Dante asserted the glory of the vulgar speech; the century of Van Artevelde, and of the fraternity on the Lake of Lucerne; the century in which the civic life stood up side by side with the chivalric life, and showed that it could contribute at least as much to the enduring spiritual and intellectual treasures of every land. It is emphatically the age in which the commons of England began to show that there could be no English people apart from them.

The fifteenth century despised its predecessor. It assumed a general European character. Battles for national and personal life, for the right to think, to speak, to breathe, are lost in projects of reconciliation, in the dream of some great republic of letters in which men of refinement shall have their own way, and be the dictators of mankind. I do not for a moment undervalue this period, or the inestimable benefits which it has bequeathed to after times. Thus, in England, it is the period which gave birth to the English public schools. If we did not participate like other nations in the great revival, if we were too busy with wars and tumults to be ready for taking much interest in Greek letters or Greek art, there was at least the soil prepared in which these might be planted and might flourish hereafter. Prelates and kings were rendering that service to coming ages, if they were ever so much inclined to blind them by the maxims of their own.

But I cannot discover that the education and the representation of the people were as much in harmony with each other—were as much acting and reacting on each other—in the Lancastrian period as in that which preceded it. The policy of the descendants of John of Gaunt was altogether unlike his. He was in sympathy with the great religious movement of the commons. At all events he saw his wisdom in favouring it. The usurping monarchs of his house saw their wisdom in crushing it, in enlisting as far as possible the ecclesiastics on their side, in making them their tools, in persecuting for them. To their period belonged two classes of statutes which would seem directly opposed to each other; the statutes for prohibiting all intercourse with Rome under the severest penalties—the statutes for burning heretics. They were really parts of the same system. One was the price paid for the other. The clergy made themselves the servants of the monarch on condition that the monarch should do their work. While this state of things was going on, the power of the House of Commons, as a mere branch of the legislature, was steadily increasing. The power of the House of Commons, as representing the true mind of the commons, was, I conceive, as steadily diminishing. Or, to speak more accurately, that mind was becoming more bewildered and unstable, losing its tone, even changing its convictions. Men who had followed Wyckliffe as the English teacher, the champion of our life and freedom against the foreigners, became a sect of Lollards, looking with discontent upon the rest of the nation, finding ever new and just reasons for complaining of ecclesiastical oppression and ecclesiastical tyranny, gradually learning to think all government and all property secular, if not devilish. The other classes were offering much justification for these opinions, whilst they had also abundant excuses for violent measures to put them down. A frightful confusion, such as could only issue in a frightful civil war; a war not of principles, or even of classes, but of adverse families, which had lost all sense of a common country, or only regarded it as fair spoil for the strongest.

Neither regal government nor parliamentary government could avert this ruin. Neither regal government nor parliamentary government could provide any adequate restoration from it. All the forms of a constitution had worked themselves out in the Plantagenet period. There were kings, lords, and commons, if the names could produce any results. But what can names avail when those who bear them are utterly unconscious of any obligation implied in them to each other, or to themselves? There are those who will say that a power was provided in this time which might redress the evils of the age, though kings and parliaments could not. The printing press was born. Surely a wonderful infant, to be received, if its descent and capacities were known, with thanksgivings and processions; to be hailed especially by those who prize what is common above what is rare, who count that more blessed which can diffuse itself everywhere, than that which can be appropriated by a few. The more one thinks of the low origin of the press, the more amazing and divine the gift appears. But we must recollect always that it is a representative, not in itself a restorative, institution. It can only exhibit what it finds. Its worth depends on the worth of that which is put into it. If a man or an age has nothing to communicate, the smaller the circumference through which that nothing spreads, the better. If a manuscript contains no life, what is the good of a machinery to diffuse it? What one hopes and believes is, that so magnificent an instrument has been revealed to men, because there are words which it is good for men of all orders to be acquainted with, which deserve the most enduring letters to set them forth, because they are meant to endure.

According to Shakespeare, the spirits of those who

had been slain in the civil wars, or by the axe of Richard, stood at the couch of Henry of Richmond, on the eve of the battle of Bosworth, to sing the advent of a new era which he was to introduce. I doubt not the spirits were right in their prediction. But, we do not, at the first contemplation of his reign, discover how it was fulfilled. Many tokens there are surely that an old and exhausted time has passed away. The factions have fought out their battle and are thoroughly wearied. There shall be no more a feudal ascendancy; the king has determined that. So far as he can determine, he will have officials who shall do his work in the best way that it can be done; men shall not do it merely because they hold certain estates, or have succeeded to certain families. The priests who are without hereditary honours, or children to whom they may leave what they hold—will they not serve the purpose best? Will they not be on the whole the most dexterous servants of the crown? Then, again, trade—ought not that to receive all encouragement? If it can be fostered, will not the glory of the mere landowner decline? Are there not signs that it is advancing itself even without our help? Has not that strange Genoese adventurer accomplished his wild project, though monarchs frowned upon it, though it looked monstrous to all judicious men? That certainly will be one of the characteristics of the new time which is coming. Will MONEY be the great power in that time? Will all things in heaven and earth bow before it?

This, perhaps, was the belief of the first Tudor king, oftentimes his most settled belief. If it should turn out to be a true belief, one may doubt whether the spirits who spoke such words of comfort to him before the battle would not have been wise to confine their messages to Richard—only to tell of the misery that had been and of the punishment which it had brought forth. In that case—if the tyranny of force in the Plantagenet period is only to be supplanted by the tyranny of gold in the Tudor—one may be sure that the representatives of the commons will represent that tyranny and the subjection to it. But there may be some other power stronger than this. It may be that both king and lords will find out that there is something stronger. Perhaps the commons will discover that they cannot be freeholders or freemen unless they confess something to be stronger. If that should be so, the spirits may yet be right. The Tudor age may burn up what is vile and refuse in the Plantagenet age, if it leaves a deposit of its own which will require to be also burnt up. It may establish what was good in the Plantagenet age, and discover some further good. The Commons' House may represent the country better than it did under the former dynasty, because it has something higher and nobler to represent. Commerce, printing, the old and new schools, the old and new literature, may all give their help towards the education of the people.

CHAPTER III.

THE HOUSE OF COMMONS IN THE TUDOR PERIOD.

A PARADOX came before us in the last chapter, to which I must again draw your attention. The friars, I said, in the reign of Henry III., appealed to the lowest masses of the land, treated them as having rights in a divine and universal society, trampled upon the pride of wealth and the exclusiveness of family. Their preaching made its way here as everywhere. After a while we perceived a vehement opposition to them. Whence did it proceed? Not from the nobles, whom it seemed to depress; but from the commons, whom it would seem to exalt. Not the dignified ecclesiastic, but the poor parsons of the town lifted their voices against maxims and practices which put contempt on riches and honoured beggary.

This contradiction explained itself to us by degrees. We found that there had always been in the Saxon churls the seeds of a national organisation, the craving for a place in the national order. They had been crushed; but the domestic life, the municipal life, had never perished in them. They had been gathering strength. The old names of the freeman and the freeholder were still dear, and were recovering something of their old force. The language of their forefathers, deepened and enriched by foreign influences, was proving its power, was subduing its conquerors. The native priests who were most in contact with the towns had shared these feelings. Their morality, their divine messages, had mingled with the sense of citizenship, had quickened it, and been quickened by it. Citizen life was felt to be a sacred life; and the man could not be separated from the good citizen. To all such belief, the friars gave a rude shock. England and its traditions were nothing to them. The family life was nothing to them. The desire of the citizen not to be a dependent on the charity of others was mocked by their own profession, which seemed to say that the greatest holiness was exhibited in this dependence. The war became fiercer day by day. The virtues and learning which distinguished a number of the friars—which have given them a wide-spread and enduring reputation—were not of the kind which the English commons could appreciate. The vices which appeared in a number of these friars came directly under their eyes, disturbed their family peace, outraged their consciences. The manliness of the citizen, his self-conceit, his respect for the money which he had saved or won, were equally scandalised by those levelling notions, in which we who look at them from a distance may see much to admire. And so the whole life and order of the English commons shaped themselves in antagonism to these instructors. Had it been a merely negative antagonism, nothing could have come of it, except insular vanity, a detestation of foreigners, an impatience of all Latin lore, a disbelief in all pretensions to faith, in all acts of sacrifice for the good of other men. But it became associated with faith, with learning, with the most genuine, unobtrusive sacrifices. The parson was celebrated by Chaucer especially in contrast to the friar, for his simple trust, for his freedom from self-indulgence, for his sympathy with the poorest of his flock. The old learning was used to provide a Bible for the people. A new native literature grew up under the shadow of it.

How much these feelings affected the House of Commons during the fourteenth century, and were kept alive by it, I endeavoured to point out. I could not overlook a change which became evident in the fifteenth. The Wyckliffite doctrines, which had influenced the commons so strongly, had also been a defence of the king's prerogative against the papal assumptions. But the Lancastrian princes disclaimed this alliance; and though as jealous as their predecessors of any Roman ascendancy, encouraged the higher ecclesiastics in putting down the followers of Wyckliffe as disturbers of the peace. A corresponding change in them became almost inevitable. Treated as a sect, they assumed the habits and title of a sect. Though still numerous, perhaps prevalent in the citizen class, they no longer appear as citizens. The contempt for property, the indifference to national life, which had been characteristic of their opponents, began to show itself in them. They continually gave their enemies an excuse for treating them as the foes of civil no less than ecclesiastical order. The Parliaments were not unwilling to pass laws against them, even to let the spiritual courts exercise their own cruel vengeance upon them.

Another phenomenon of the opposite kind was seen, not in England but in Italy, at the close of the fifteenth and the beginning of the sixteenth century. A Dominican monk appeared not merely as the impugner of ecclesiastical luxury and oppression—that would have been in harmony with the earliest traditions of his order—but as the organiser of a city; as the champion of civic freedom. The story of Savonarola in Florence may be claimed by Dominicans as a testimony that if they have sometimes been signalised as persecutors, there is a side of their minds which is in strong sympathy with freedom, and which treats it as inseparable from faith and morality. One would rejoice that any of them should vindicate that part of their heritage. If Protestants are jealous of their pretensions, they may discover in the weaknesses of the great Florentine preacher, how much Italian freedom suffered in his hands through his estrangement from those domestic ties out of which the life of the citizen unfolds itself.

We had no Florence in England, and we could have no Savonarola—least of all in the Tudor period. For that was a time when separate cities were becoming more and more merged in the whole nation; when the central power of the king was becoming greater than it had ever been. The family factions had worn themselves out. Henry VII., I remarked before, was fully resolved not to be merely the first baron of his realm. To all appearance he might become a merely arbitrary sovereign; using the new instrument which commerce and civilization had put into his hands, using his own dexterity, to rob the country of its native strength, whilst he professed only to be uprooting its feudalism. He was in no sympathy with the Commons, except as being the enemy of the nobles; that which had been most strong in them he would keep down to please the ecclesiastics who were his servants. He did not care much for the old learning or for the new.

Henry VIII. was surely not disposed to be less a king than his father. But a greater geniality, a preference of ostentation to the amassing of money, a love for the old learning as well as the new, made an amazing difference in his influence upon all classes of his people. Many springs which had been dried up must have been let loose at his accession. The chief minister might not be popular with nobles or commons; but he had caught the splendour of the popes, who believed that they might rule Christendom by being heads of a commonwealth of letters. He would raise universities; he suspected that monasteries had done their work; he knew, at all events, that they needed reformation. A reformation, doubtless, he would have been well disposed to give the land; such a reformation as scholars would have thought sufficient then, as many of them would prefer to that which actually took place now. I apprehend his reformation would have stirred no depths of human thought and belief, and could therefore have really redressed no great abuses. It would have added to the surface of English civilization; it would have removed some of the absurdities which Erasmus had exposed; it would have made corruptions less odious and glaring. But it would have left the commons much as it found them; it would not have brought out the heart and life of the English citizen. That reformation, which was not shaped according to man's speculations, but according to God's order, was strictly national. It did not, indeed, begin from us. The spark which was lighted in one of the cities of the empire was that which blazed up in our land; yet the king who denounced Luther, and whom Luther denounced—the king who to the last had no sympathy with his followers or with him—was the centre of the movement. The men who had most entered into Luther's mental conflict, who clung most to his watchword, looked on the king as their champion, even when they had most excuse for suspecting him as their tyrant.

When King Henry asserted his supremacy and cast off the pope's supremacy, we often say that he broke through the traditions of centuries. Undoubtedly Sir Thomas More felt so; perhaps the king felt so himself, since he had within a few years identified the cause of the monarchs of Europe with the cause of their spiritual father. And yet he was also *maintaining* the traditions of centuries. Sir Thomas More could not have denied that he was walking in the steps of his Norman and Plantagenet fathers, if he had gone one step beyond them. Henry must have often strengthened himself by precedents drawn from their doings and their maxims, even when he seemed to be most departing from his own. But how could he take that one step in advance of them? how could he actually cut the thread which they had been continually trying to untie? Because it was no longer a contest of king against pope; because there was a strong conviction in the land which demanded the severance of the tie as being a greater bondage upon people than upon kings. When I use the phrase "strong conviction," I do not mean the conviction of a majority, I do not mean the conviction of the highest men in the land. Very few laymen or ecclesiastics in the upper stations of society were possessed by it; if the poor of the land had been polled, they would unquestionably have been on the side of the convents. It might have been said, it was said, by many an ecclesiastic, that the passion for reform dwelt only in a few students of the universities, whose heads had been turned by reading the Dialogues of Erasmus, or listening to his lectures on the Greek Testament; by some who had caught the Wittemberg fever, by a few Lollards of the towns, whose fathers and grandfathers had heard Wyckliffe's Bible read out of MS. copies, who had themselves evaded the vigilance of the courts by obtaining it in print. The calculation of the priests about the insignificance of the voices from which the cry against them arose was correct —only two items were overlooked in it. One was the fact that the cry arose out of human spirits, which must obtain deliverance in some way from fetters with which they were sure that men and not God had bound them; the other was that these men, however little they understood each other—to whatever different classes or schools they belonged—really expressed the mind of the English *nation*, not of any sect or school. And therefore they could range themselves with no sect or school. They might be passing through the very agonies of conscience which Luther had passed through, but they were not Lutherans. Some of them might have learnt much through Wyckliffe, but they were not Wyckliffites. The king, who hated sects and foreign innovations, and was shaking off a foreign yoke, was their natural head. Him they could recognise as God's own gift to them. He was the point of union which they required. He made them *feel* that they were champions for the nation against its oppressors. His faith might not be theirs, but their faith sustained him. He might suspect, even persecute, those who cherished their creed. Still they were sure that it was a faithful act—a protest against the most unpatriotic and immoral tendencies of the Church—to claim him rather than any favourite preacher or doctor as their leader.

In the memorable year 1529, the House of Commons led the movement which issued in the greatest acts of reformation. How their sympathy with the king developed their own strength and freedom— how great the difference is between a House which merely goes through the trade of meeting and legislating, and one which represents a strong conviction, I do not know where we can better learn than in the following passage from Mr. Froude's first volume. After quoting from Hall an account of the opening of the Parliament, the first after the fall of Wolsey, and after giving the oration in which the Chancellor, Sir Thomas More, standing on the right hand of the king, set forth the causes for which he had summoned them, the writer remarks :

" The world was changing; how swiftly, how completely no one knew ; but a confusion no longer tolerable was a patent fact to all men, and with a wise instinct it was wished that the grievances of the nation, which had accumulated through centuries, should be submitted to complete ventilation, without reserve, check, or secrecy. For this purpose it was essential that the House should not be interfered with, that they should be allowed full liberty to express their wishes, and to act upon them. Accordingly, the practice usual with ministers of undertaking the direction of the proceedings was clearly on this occasion foregone. In the House of Commons, then as much as now, there was in theory unrestricted liberty of discussion, and free right for every member to originate whatever motion he pleased. 'The discussions in the English Parliament,' writes Henry himself to the Pope, 'are free and unrestricted; the Crown has no power to limit their debating, or to control the votes of their members. They determine everything for themselves, as the interests of the commonwealth require.' But," Mr. Froude goes on, " when there was confidence between the Crown and the people, these rights were in a great measure surrendered. The ministers proposed the business which was to be transacted; and the temper of the House was usually so well understood that, except when there was a demand for money, it was rarely that a measure was proposed, the acceptance of which was doubtful, or the nature of which could provoke debate. So little jealousy or dread was in quiet times entertained of the power of the Crown, and so little was a residence in London to the taste of the burgess or the country gentleman, that not only were their expenses defrayed by a considerable salary, but it was found necessary to forbid their absenting themselves from the duties by a positive enactment." ("History of England," vol. i., pp. 187, 188.)

That enactment was passed in the sixth year of

Henry. Mark the difference between that and the twentieth year:

"In the composition of the House of Commons, which had now assembled, no symptoms appeared of such indifference. The election had taken place in the midst of great and general excitement, and the men who were chosen, if we may judge from their acts and their petitions, were men of that broad, resolved temper who, only in times of popular effervescence, are called forth into prominence. It would probably have been impossible for the Crown to attempt dictation or repression at such a time, if it had desired to do so. Under the actual circumstances its interest was to encourage the fullest expression of public feeling" (p. 188).

I cannot extract the long petition "To the king, our sovereign lord," which contained their statement of public grievances. It is one of the great documents for the history of this period, and would illustrate many points of which I have been speaking. But it would draw us away from the business which I have now in hand. I wish you to see first how the moral feeling in the country, the sense of immoral abuses which must be removed, produced an altogether new energy in the House of Commons; next, how this energy served to unite instead of to sever the different parts of the constitution; how it caused the king and the commons to realise their relation to each other, as they had never realised it. We may take in this lesson without accepting the favourable opinion of Henry's character to which the eminent historian I have just quoted has given the weight of his knowledge and judgment. We may, if we please, hold fast to the old notion that he was a self-willed tyrant; the facts will remain the same on that hypothesis; and it will be all the more wonderful, that, in spite of such a disposition, and in the very acts which might seem to gratify it most, he rendered such homage to the mind of the country and to the spirit as well as the form of its institutions. After considering what Mr. Froude has said so ingeniously and ably about the executions of Sir Thomas More, Ann Boleyn, and Cromwell—fully admitting also that he is more in accordance with Shakespeare than the more recent opinion is, and giving great weight to the testimony of Michelet, who cannot be suspected of Anglican partialities, that Henry was the most straightforward and honest of all the monarchs of his time—I yet feel unable to overcome my old prejudices, or to understand how the example of the king's domestic conduct can have been otherwise than most injurious to the land. Yet I do perceive that he became, by the very necessity of his position, such an instructor of his people as no sovereign since the conquest had been. He was imbued, as I said before, with the old education and the new. He had been trained in the theology and the logic of the schools, he had delighted in the conversation of his chancellor, and had entertained Erasmus. Both kinds of knowledge were equally foreign to the habits of the

English citizen. The king's ambition to display the first had made him an anti-reformer. If he had yielded to the second he would have become a mere dilettante, after the model of Francis I. But the mixture of the two, the conflict of the two in his mind, after he had thrown off the papal yoke, while it often gave the most inconsistent appearance to his own opinions, helped to counteract a number of tendencies that would have been mischievous to his subjects, and to develop what was most vital and most strong in them. The king was inclined to be a theological dogmatist. But his dogmatism could not assume a settled form of opposition to the papist or to the reformer. He was ready to curse each in turn; he really gave play to the thoughts and energies of each. He was obliged to accept the work which they could do in raising the mind of the citizen, in making him a healthier and more useful man, as the test of their divinity. And it is striking to observe how willingly the most distinguished men of the time, though nursed in controversy, though full of the keenest spirit of controversy, submitted to this test. They must give signs of their own power to endure it — they must show that their opponent cannot endure it. The complaints which the reformers make of abuses in doctrine or practice must take the form of showing that the doctrines were unable to form good fathers, sons, brothers, subjects, or that their promoters set up some artificial inhuman standard of worth instead of this. The Romanist advocates charged them with injuring Christianity by overthrowing ancient traditions, and by substituting faith for good works. The answer was, that there were moral commandments of God, which were older than traditions, and that the works which they disparaged were *not* good. Both parties staked their credit on the results of their teaching, upon its power to form a people.

No person illustrates the position of one party in this time so well as Hugh Latimer. In the reign of Henry, after he had been made Bishop of Worcester, he preached a Latin sermon to his brethren in convocation. It is on the children of this world, who wish to keep all things dark, and the children of light, whose function is to spread light. The preacher is quite aware that his hearers would say, "The lay people, with the king at their head, are the children of this world; we are of the other class." He does not the least encourage them in that delusion. In the following reign he translated his sermon, " to the intent that things well said to a few may be understood of many, and do good to all those who desire to understand the truth." So that I may give his own nervous English:—

" The end of your convocation shall show what ye have done ; the fruit that shall come of your consultation shall show what generation ye be of. For what have ye done hitherto, I pray you, these seven years and more? What have ye engendered? What have ye brought forth ? What fruit is come of your long and great assembly? What are they that the people of England have been the better of a hair? or you yourselves either made accepted before God, or better discharged towards the people committed unto your care? For that the people is better learned and taught now, to whether of these ought we to attribute it: to your industry, or to the providence of God and the foreseeing of the king's grace? Ought we to thank you or the king's highness? Whether stirred other first: you the king, that he might preach; or he you, by his letters, that ye should preach oftener? Is it unknown, think you, that both ye and your curates were, in a manner, by violence, forced to let books to be made, not by you, but by profane and lay persons—to let them, I say, be sold abroad, and read for the instruction of the people? I am bold with you; but I speak Latin and not English—to the clergy, not to the laity. I speak to you being present, and not behind your backs. God is my witness, I speak whatsoever is spoken of the good-will that I bear you. God is my witness, which knoweth my heart, and compelleth me to say that I say."

These words were spoken, as Latimer says, in the face of the clergy, and not behind their backs; still we might fancy that he was seeking favour with the sovereign at the expense of his brethren. There is a letter of Master Latimer's to King Henry VIII., "for restoring again the free liberty of reading the Holy Scriptures," which will certainly save him from this imputation. It will show, that if it was a time when men of the commons trusted in their king, it was not a time when they crouched to him with any cowardice:

"Here I beseech your grace to pardon me a while, and patiently to hear me a word or two; yea, though it be so as concerning your high majesty and regal power, wherewith Almighty God hath called your grace. There is as great a difference between you and me as between God and man; for you be here to me, and to all your subjects, in God's stead, to defend, aid, and succour us in our right, and so I should tremble and quake to speak to your grace. But again, as concerning that you are a mortal man, in danger of sin, having in you the corrupt nature of Adam, in the which all we are both conceived and born, so have you no less need of the merit of Christ's passion for your salvation than I and other of your subjects have, which be all members of the mystical body of Christ. And, though you be a higher member, yet must you not disdain the lesser; for, as St. Paul saith, those members which are taken to be most vile and had in least reputation, be as necessary as the other for the preservation and keeping of the body. This, most gracious king, when I considered, and also your favourable and gentle nature, I was bold to write this bold, homely, and simple letter unto your grace, trusting that you will accept my true and faithful mind even as it is."

The object of the letter is to fight against those "who boast themselves to be guides and captains unto others, and challenge unto themselves the knowledge of Holy Scripture, yet will neither show the truth themselves, as they be bound, neither suffer them that would." " They will," he says, " as much as in them lieth, debar not only the Word of God, which David calleth a light to direct and show every man how to order his affections and lusts according to the commandments of God, but also by their subtle wiliness they instruct, move, and provoke in a manner all kings in Christendom, to aid, succour, and help them in this their mischief. And especially in this your realm, they have blinded your liege people and subjects with their laws, customs, ceremonies, and Banbury glosses, and punished them with curses, excommunications, and other corruptions — corrections, I would say. And now, at the last, when they see that they cannot prevail against the open truth, which, the more it is persecuted the more it increaseth by their tyranny, they have made it treason to your noble grace to have the Scripture in English!"

This was the Reformers' battle. They invoked the king's help on the side of the citizen. They urged him as a king to uphold domestic morality and civil order; to put forth the Bible as the defender of both; to put down superstitions which undermined both. As long as they could not call the monarch the patron of their cause—while they could only reason with him as a king—so long, I believe, every day's experience gave new force to their arguments; if some of the bishops persecuted, Latimer could avouch that "the truth increaseth more by their tyrannies."

But the time arrived when the Reformers had a king whom they *could* claim as a patron; when they had license from his council to persecute; when the destruction of that which had been dear and sacred in the eyes of the people became a fashion. Then the other party could bring forth their reasons with the greatest effect; then they could produce evidence —to me it appears indisputable evidence—that the morality of the land had been shaken, that the citizen had turned the new doctrine into a reason for his own ill doings and a license for slandering and despising his neighbour. Mr. Froude quotes from Foxe a remonstrance of Gardiner's at the beginning of the reign of Edward VI., of which he says that "it was not recommended by the maker of it, but was not the less wise in itself." Most men who are not partisans will, I should think, agree with this judgment. And, considering the language in which later defenders of Romanism have spoken of Henry, it is curious to hear the great champion of it in that day saying, when he had no longer any fear of his frown or hope from his smiles, that "for himself he would rather be wrong with Plato than right with the others; and that if, as some alleged, Henry had but one eye, and saw not God's truth perfectly, he had rather go to heaven with one eye after him, than travel for another eye with danger to lose both."

Such testimonies may go very little way in settling

our judgment about a historical character. But they go a great way in showing how much a king might do to give the different influences which were working in the commonwealth a national and not a party character; how much he might remind each party of the end for which it professed to exist. I certainly feel that the bishop with whom I have the least sympathy did something which the one with whom I have most sympathy could not do; their common allegiance to the king and their common respect for him was the bond which held them together, when each would have deemed that he was doing good service in exterminating the other.

A higher ruler than Henry did not permit the Reformers or the Romanists to effect that object, though each in turn was permitted to try what it could do. Most humiliating to the victorious party was the experiment in the reign of Edward VI. I do not dwell here upon the other crimes of that reign, which have been so honestly and admirably illustrated in Mr. Froude's account of it. I wish to fix your minds on one subject which directly concerns the business of these Lectures, which has forced itself upon us already, and which will occupy us more and more as we proceed. That a people must be organic —that an inorganic mass, though we may carelessly and even with a very good purpose, give it that name, can never vindicate it for itself—this has been the maxim from which I started, and of which I hope not to lose sight. That there is always a tendency in those who are organised to prevent the entrance of any who lie beyond their circle within it, and that a severe penalty awaits their selfishness; that they put in peril the position which they have achieved, and incur the danger of sinking themselves into an undistinguished mass; these are lessons which the Roman history taught us, and which have been repeated in various passages of our own. And now came a critical moment, when they would be directly connected with the history of the Reformation. The citizen has maintained his rights against the friar. The mere glorification of poverty has been put down. Beggary has become discreditable. The yeoman and the freeman of the town have asserted their dignity. They have their own House, their veritable representative, which has proved that it is mightier than the old baronial House, which has co-operated with the king in a work to which that House would not have been inclined. The citizen has had his own minister, his Thomas Cromwell, who, in spite of the jealousy of nobles, in spite of the opposition of a mighty and aged corporation, has overthrown the monasteries—the nobles being then, by a policy for which some person or other is answerable, bribed by the spoils of the convents to acquiesce in the new system, and dread any return to the old. And now the reformer can boast that all is proceeding according to his pleasure. His enemies are humbled; the young king is wholly on his side; he may mock and persecute those who mocked and persecuted him.

The story would be too old a one to point any special moral, if there were not the ghastly fact that there were multitudes of poor who were not citizens, who were not cared for any longer, of whom some account must be taken, who must destroy the new order of things if it could not, in some way, deal with them. This terrific problem begins to stare the reformers of the reign of Edward VI. in the face. They know that to go back is impossible. The friars have been weighed in the balances, and found wanting; the citizens have conquered them. The convents cannot be recalled into existence to feed the beggars at their doors; that business is evidently obsolete. But the disease is not the less appalling because these remedies are clearly inapplicable. It confronts the best teachers of the land in the moment of their exultation. It makes them utterly ashamed; for they not only see that there is another class to provide for which lies beyond the sacred enclosure: those who are within that enclosure, the class of the freemen, are losing their position, are sinking to a lower level. Hear Latimer on this point. He is a man who must speak truth at all times, and before all persons. He is now preaching before King Edward, as he did before the Convocation :—" My father was a yeoman, and had no lands of his own; only he had a farm of three or four pounds by the year at the uttermost, and hereupon he tilled so much as kept half a dozen men. He had walks for a hundred sheep; and my mother milked thirty kine. He was able, and did find the king a harness, with himself and his horse, while he came to the place that he should receive the king's wages. I can remember that I buckled his horse when he came to Blackheath field. He kept me to school, or else I had not been able to have preached before the king's majesty now. He married my sisters with five pounds, or twenty nobles, apiece; so that he brought them up in godliness and the fear of God. He kept hospitality to his poor neighbours, and some alms he gave to the poor. And all this he did off the said farm, when he who now hath it payeth sixteen pound by year or month, is not able to do anything for his friends, nor for himself, nor for his children, or give a cup of drink to the poor. Thus all the enhancing and rearing goeth to your private commodity and wealth. So that where ye had a single too much, you have that; and since the same, ye have enhanced the rent, and so have increased another too much; so now you have double too much. But let the preacher preach till his tongue be worn to the stumps, nothing is amended. We have good statutes made for the commonwealth as touching commoners and enclosures; many meetings and sessions; but in the end of the matter there cometh nothing forth. Well, well, this is one thing I will say unto you; from whence it cometh I know, even from the devil. I know his intent in it. For if ye bring it to pass that the yeomanry be not able to put their sons to school (as indeed universities do wondrously decay already), and that they be not able to marry their daughters to the avoiding of whoredom; I say ye pluck salvation from the people, and utterly destroy the realm. For by yeomen's sons the faith of Christ is and hath been maintained chiefly. Is this realm taught by rich men's sons? No, no; read the chroniclers; ye shall find sometimes noblemen's sons which have been unpreaching bishops and prelates, but ye shall find none of them learned men. But verily they that should look to the redressing of these things be the greatest against them. In this realm are a great many folks, and amongst many, I know but one of tender zeal who at the motion of his poor tenants hath let down his lands to the old rents for their relief. For God's love let him not be a phœnix, let him not be alone, let him not be a hermit closed in a wall; one good man follow, and do as he giveth example. Surveyors there be that greedily gorge up their food; hand-makers, I mean; they make up their mouth, but the commons be utterly undone by them; whose bitter cry ascending up to the ears of the Lord of Sabaoth, the greedy pit of hell-burning fire, without great repentance, doth tarry and look for them. A redress God grant! For surely but that two things do comfort me, I would despair of redress in these matters. One is that the king's majesty, when he cometh to age, will see a redress of these things, so out of frame; giving example by letting down his own lands first, and then enjoin his subjects to follow him. The second hope I have is, I believe that the general accounting day is at hand—the dreadful day of judgment I mean, which shall make an end of all these calamities and miseries."

So spoke this great Reformer, this yeoman's son, in the days when his own party was in the ascendant, when Protestantism had apparently beaten down all its foes. Here and elsewhere Latimer, instead of singing pæans for that victory, labours to turn it to some account by fairly counting out the losses as well as the gains of the conflict, and by warning his friends that if they had won for themselves, and hoped to gain honour and spoils for themselves, there would be a curse upon their banners, whatever grand names and watchwords might be inscribed upon them. To us, looking back upon the reign of Edward from this distance, it seems as if the two permanent fruits which had survived its crimes and miseries, had been, first, this great lesson, next the witness which it bore that a common worship is a bond for the subjects of a land which theories are seeking to divide; that such worship may find its expression in words composed in earlier ages by men who spoke different languages, and looked at the universe from very different points of view; that it should, however, be rendered into a dialect which all members of a nation can recognise as their own.

The ignominious acts of Edward's reign, the debasement of the coinage, the wretchedness of its factions, only bring forth the worth of this testimony, and of that which was borne by such faithful men as

Latimer, into greater brilliancy. They make us feel how true the anticipation of the honest preacher was, that a judgment was approaching the land—whatever confused notions he might have about the nature of that judgment; a judgment which would sift men of all professions, and through which only such as he would pass safely.

Certainly the reign of Mary was as great an evidence as that of her father's had been, how little the English people will ever endure the rule of a sect—call that sect by what name you please; how it turns to any sovereign who has legal and hereditary claims upon its allegiance as a protection from that rule. The conscience of the English citizen, as much as of the noble—the conscience of the whole people—revolted against the scheme of Northumberland to substitute his excellent kinswoman for the daughter of Catherine. It was not merely the selfishness of the project which made it hateful, not merely the suspicion of utter hypocrisy in its author. There was a deep, genuine, national conviction that the Protestant preachers and nobles were endeavouring to set aside God's order for their order. Every charge which they had brought against Papists came back with tremendous force upon themselves. It was a miserable pretence that they were sacrificing merely secular arrangements to the paramount claims of faith. None had affirmed so strongly as they had done that all such calculations were unlawful and unbelieving. They were proving that their belief was in themselves, in *their* secular arrangements, not in the government of God at all. Such a contradiction had its necessary fruit in a vehement reaction—a reaction in which the whole land participated—a reaction which was visible in the House that represented the commons, the only part of the legislature, indeed, wherein it could be conspicuously visible, since it was the only part which had entered heartily into the Reformation. The reaction, up to the point which it reached, cannot be imputed to them, or to the people of England generally, as an inconsistency. The Reformation had been a protest for national order. If it lost that character, the sympathy which accompanied it was not strangely or unnaturally withdrawn. There were persons among the clergy, as well as the nobles, who consciously deserted their faith, or who showed that it had never been their faith at all. One cannot say so of the body of the people, or of any integral part of that body. It adhered, on the whole, to the conviction with which it had started. The national flag—that which bore the sovereign's name upon it —was dear to the heart of the Englishman. What other characters there were upon it he read but indistinctly. He might be told, by one party or another, that they were sacred characters. Now and then, some flash of light might show him that they were. But it was the king who spoke to him of the King of kings, confusedly enough no doubt, very often; but more clearly, so as to convey a greater

THE TWO REACTIONS. 91

sense of trust in a living person, than any opinions which divines might entertain or inculcate.

It was therefore the proof which such men as Latimer, Ridley, Rogers, Hooper gave, that they were believing in an actual person, to whom they were not afraid to trust themselves in life or death— not in some subtle points of divinity or casuistry— which was the great instrument of stopping this reaction and producing another. The test which had been applied in Henry's reign was still the effectual one in Mary's. What are your methods of making good citizens? How do you hope to give the queen faithful and obedient subjects? Mary's counsellors answered, "Here is our method; we think this the most effectual." It did not seem so to the English commons. They had entertained no very high standard of human excellence. The comfortable man, the man who could make money and keep it, had for them many of the tokens of the man of worth. But they were capable of acknowledging higher worth than this. A powerful demonstration might establish the belief in the stubborn English heart that there were men who could give up money, respectability, life, rather than tell a lie. The demonstration would not have been effectual if the men who made this sacrifice had despised the earth, if they had been indifferent to domestic ties. But the Marian reformers had wives and children, boasted of them, counted them a part of their religion. Even these proofs might have failed, if Mary's persecutions had not been accompanied with other acts, which destroyed altogether the thought that she was a national sovereign. The Spanish marriage went some way towards removing that prestige from her character, even though there might be good reason to believe that Philip did not kindle, but rather tried to abate, the fires of Smithfield. And if the dream of England's being reduced into a province of Spain haunted the mind of the commons, the submission to Rome, which Pole considered more important than all suppression of Protestant opinions, was more directly an affront to the national feeling than that suppression could be. It became strangely complicated through the Pope's personal hostility to his greatest defender. And that hostility again brought out the sovereign in something of the special Tudor character, as an asserter of her own authority against the ecclesiastical authority.

Strangely, therefore, as this reign is contrasted with the next, there was the closest connexion between them; the one was the natural precursor of the other. We may entertain the most various opinions about the character of Elizabeth, as we do about the character of her father. The same person may be conscious of often changing his opinions about it as it has presented itself to him in different lights and in different periods. New evidence may sometimes shake old conclusions. But on the whole the impression that is left in our minds by the literature of the period remains. The queen is the centre of the time. The vicissitudes of her opinions, the changes in her affections, are not only necessary to the history, they even help to make it intelligible. After considering Edward's reign and Mary's, we feel that her uncertainty, whether she was a Protestant or a Catholic, was what determined her position as a national sovereign, was what gave the whole reign so intensely national a character. The queen was neither Romanist nor Protestant, was both Romanist and Protestant; for that was the condition of her subjects. She was not indifferent to either faith—there was no indifference in the time. There was earnestness in the support of each conviction in those who clung to each, a vehement Protestantism, a vehement Romanism; there was also a sense in the strongest minds, in those who most set forth this time to all times—in Spenser and Shakespeare, as well as in Hooker—of some meeting-point which there must be, of something imperfect in each, unless it has the aid and support of the other. The habit of the age was to exaggerate the worth and grandeur of the queen, as if she were herself the reconciler; as if in rallying round her there was a sufficient protest against foreign aggression, against the glorification of particular opinions, which the heart of the nation demanded. It was a temper which had been manifesting itself through all the Tudor reigns, which reached its climax and consummation in the last. Throughout, the House of Commons had been a tolerably faithful index of it. The opinions of the Lords had been influenced by various causes. In them was seen much adherence to the old habits and tendencies, qualified by some personal dislike of ecclesiastics, and by unwillingness to surrender the revenues which they had won from ecclesiastical corporations. The House of the freeholders and the freemen, less affected by these disturbing influences, was a more exact barometer of the feeling, not only of those who elected it, but of the country at large. It adhered in general to its Plantagenet traditions. It suspected the higher ecclesiastics, chiefly as not being thoroughly English in their tastes and sympathies. Protestantism was valued so far as it was opposed to foreign practices; the sovereign, male and female, was dear as the protector against priestly ascendancy and continental usurpation. With these fundamental principles, all changes which appeared merely to affect opinion were compatible; efforts to define opinion were not understood, or regarded as specially necessary, unless they could be used as tests of fidelity to the national order.

This state of things, especially this sympathy of the Crown with the House of Commons, was to be rudely shaken in the coming period. There were signs before the close of Elizabeth's reign that the powers which had worked harmoniously together might become antagonists. Hitherto the reverence for charters and precedents, as a protection against the sovereign, has belonged peculiarly to the nobles. It may become the great characteristic of the commons; the watchwords of Prerogative and Privilege may mingle with all the religious questions with which the Tudor time has been occupied.

That this time has left some enormous questions unsolved, which would torment subsequent generations, we have had evident proofs. The peasants' war in Germany perplexed Martin Luther with the strangest doubts. The farmer class, the citizen class, had responded to his words; he was sure that he had done something for their emancipation, if they would only take up their freedom. Here was a class which said that he had not emancipated them; which had the wildest conceptions of a divine power that could emancipate them. There was not a similar struggle in England; but there were the rumblings of the storm. There were tokens that the peasants here, as little as there, were satisfied with what the Reformation had done for them; that they even suspected it of doing them mischief. These, too, were surely men; interested in any redemption that had been made for men. The friars had said so. Were the reformed teachers unable or unwilling to recognise the claim?

But if the Tudor period left this knot for other generations to untie, it has borne fruit, which after generations have gathered and fed on. The money god, whom Henry VII. worshipped, had abundance of homage from his successors. Sovereigns and priests, lords and commons, offered sacrifices and poured out incense at his shrine. He tasted the human blood, which he loves. But it had been shown that he is not the Lord of Lords. He had been defied in his high places. From the day that Luther put forth his theses against the sale of indulgences, popes have been admonished, to their great astonishment, that money is not the instrument for remitting sins. The king who deprives himself of the authority which the Pope's sanction gives him, must appeal to another power than the money power to keep his subjects in obedience. The book which was written by fishermen and a tentmaker, which says that it is hard for rich men to enter into the kingdom of God, which declares one who passed as a carpenter's son to have all power in heaven and earth, must go forth as the argument from the king that the land owes Him, as he owes it, all loyal service. The lords may exchange military duties for rents paid in coin; but if that is their only bond to their tenants, preachers will bear witness to them—facts will bear witness to them—that a judgment of God must one day rend that frail bond asunder. The freeholder and the freeman often fancy that the gold which is the reward of their industry is the standard by which they themselves, as well as the things they buy and sell, is to be measured. The dishonesty of statesmen, the selfishness of preachers, strengthen the delusion. But they also help to scatter it. The standard is found to be an utterly precarious one; any caprice subverts it; a revolution causes the riches to make themselves wings and fly from their possessors. The men who can part with them, who can throw away themselves, are the strong men. By them the hearts and minds of the commons are roused and moulded. Whatever energy there is in the House of Commons to assert freedom for the land is learned from these. So far as this influence triumphs over the money influence, the House is an instrument of preserving what is best in their constituents—of delivering them from what is worst. So far as it succumbs to the money influence, it represents the baseness of the constituency; it perpetuates its baseness to the generations that are to follow. These are some of the lessons of the Tudor period. Will the Stuarts confirm or reverse them?

CHAPTER IV.

THE HOUSE OF COMMONS IN THE STUART PERIOD.

A PEOPLE must consist of freemen; this, we found, was a maxim of the Roman; this has been our English maxim. It may become in practice a very exclusive maxim; the number of the free may be small, the number of the unfree may be great. The free may do their utmost to exclude the unfree from rising to the same position with them. But the distinction must be kept in mind amidst all changes in the condition of one class or another. It is never more important than in the Stuart period. The greatest questions of our history are involved in it, and become hopelessly intricate if we forget it. And it affected the history of the settlement of the North American colonies; the earliest and the latest events in their life are only intelligible in the light of it.

I observed that our best writers had not always adhered consistently to this use of the word "people." Shakespeare departs from it in his Roman plays. He makes it sometimes represent those who were asking

THE HISTORICAL DRAMA.

for freedom, not those who had attained it. There was a special difficulty in the time of Elizabeth in finding a name to express that great body of poor for whom the celebrated law of her reign made a provision. The words "serf" and "slave" were becoming odious in themselves, and were entirely inapplicable to this class. The serf or the slave is dependent upon some master; these were recognised as under the care of the state. It was bound to take account of them, at least not to let them starve. Again, to call these the "commons" would have been a great offence. The commons were a substantive recognised part of the commonwealth. They were emphatically the freemen and the freeholders. They were represented in a House which was every day feeling itself more and more the steward for that age of an inheritance which had descended from other ages.

The sense of this inheritance was a characteristic of the Elizabethan life and literature. If Shakespeare had some trouble in finding a name to denote those who were not yet organised, no one realised more strongly the continuance from age to age of a people which had been organised. No country possesses such a treasure as the historical plays. I do not speak of the genius exhibited in them, except so far as his genius enabled him to perceive a real divine drama working itself out through some of the most confused, even some of the dullest, passages in our annals. I speak of the assurance which they give us that the England of Henry VIII. was the same as the England of John, in spite of all the changes and convulsions which it had undergone. I speak of the witness which they bear to the intimate relation between the life of the king and the life of the whole land. That characteristic they derive from Shakespeare's Elizabethan education. He could not have had it if he had been born in the reign of James. He could not have retained it if he had caught the complexion of that period. He might have picked out some pretty story of Prince Arthur's murder by his uncle. He might have introduced a set of Gadshill pickpockets about Prince Harry. These might have been admired as the cunning inventions of a clever artist; the stage might have welcomed them. But they would have been no helps in understanding the reigns of King John or Henry IV. In the actual play, the boy Arthur helps to link together the history of conflicts of feudal kings with each other and with the citizens of the towns—of struggles between the king and the pope, the king and his barons. The Gadshill pickpockets enabled us to apprehend one aspect of a confused period, all the aspects of which are presented with equal fidelity, and illuminate each other; so that no errors of costume hinder us from feeling that the picture is in conformity not only with the general laws of humanity, but with the special conditions of the time which it brings before us.

It is impossible to find any hero in any of these plays except the king. Let him be as contemptible as John, as feeble as Richard II. or Henry VI., still he is the centre of all the movements of the drama, all the persons and events dispose themselves naturally about him. The poet cannot choose his favourite, he must follow what he perceives to be the actual order of things. For Elizabeth, as we have seen, whatever she was, held this position in the eyes of her subjects. They could not frame the scheme of their lives without reference to her. She may discourage piracies on the Spaniards, but Drake commits them in her name, and for her glory. She may not in the least understand Raleigh's enterprises, but Virginia must testify of her presence. She may look with a cold eye on the great strife in the Low Countries, but Sidney fights and dies that she may be associated with their freedom. You cannot penetrate into the fairy realm without finding that she marshals the knights, assigns them their adventures, dispenses their crowns.

It was impossible that this state of things should continue. It survives in the noblest literature; but it was becoming fantastic; there must be a change. It came very suddenly. To all appearance literature would not suffer from it. That was to receive all manner of patronage. James would pay it an honour which Elizabeth had never paid it. No man with the temper of Burleigh should hinder the distribution of his favours to those who could produce great books. The king would certainly be the centre of a set of wise men; what better government could there be than one of which they should be the chief counsellors?

Dr. Johnson may have had excuses for ridiculing the pompous line of one of his contemporaries—

"Who rules free people must himself be free;"

but certainly the case of James I. strengthens it more than it can be weakened by the cleverest parody. The unfree king is the description that might fit him better than any other. All classes in the country must have felt it. The noble who connected freedom with manly bearing and courage—to whom the word Frank was so nearly a synonym with free—saw a man utterly without grace, trembling at a sword, practised yet not skilful in evasions, cultivating chicanery. Such a spectacle, one would have thought, must have been more painful to the great lords than to any other part of the community, especially as it was connected with a king who here, as in Scotland, poured out his favours on ignoble parasites. But though those who frequented the court might see most of the king's weakness, and might ridicule it most, they were not the persons whom his acts and his mode of thinking scandalised most. Men who never came near the person of the sovereign had often a much profounder loyalty than those who could complain of his slights and criticise his manners. The freeholders of the counties, even the freemen of the towns, would have liked to think of their monarch as the model of British chivalry, as the champion of British dignity in every country of Europe. They were forced to think of him as one who disliked the name they bore, who had no notion of any order of society but one consisting of clans, who thought that the king represented the majesty of God, and *therefore* was to be always on the watch against the liberty of his people.

It was this conviction of the unfree king which introduced what must be called the age of the House of Commons—the age when it was driven into a position of direct antagonism to the monarch—the age when it represented the freedom which he counted it the main function of his kingcraft to counteract and abridge. We naturally turn to the most stirring part of this struggle—to the battle of the next reign. But it is only intelligible when we consider the commencement of it, and connect that with some of the peculiarities of the first Stuart.

It was the melancholy fortune of two sets of men that James made himself their patron, and that they became his allies and worshippers. The first were the bishops and the dignified clergy of the English Church. They had trembled at his Presbyterian education and oaths, at his Roman Catholic mother. To find him utterly renouncing the first, with the most undoubted sincerity, with a passionate loathing; to find him proving the Pope to be Antichrist in his books, and, at least after the Gunpowder Plot, prepared heartily to persecute his adherents—this was a surprise and a triumph which might easily turn the heads of well-disposed men, convinced that they were maintaining the true line of peace and moderation against enemies on both sides. It did lead to some of the most humiliating exhibitions of which there is any record—to a tacit, often an expressed, agreement. —" Since you identify your prerogative with the maintenance of our order, we will enter into a war, defensive and offensive, on behalf of it ;"—to this agreement, and thence to a real persuasion, that the cause of the Church and of freedom were hostile causes ; that the influence of the one must be used to subvert the other.

The second class which was to undergo perilous honours and grievous transformation through the influence of the Stuart king was that to which I alluded before. Men of letters were becoming, more than they had ever been before, a profession, or guild, or freemasons' lodge, with James as their grand-master. That Atticus was he who prepared and sealed this compact; that Bacon represents the submission of scholars and men of science to the royal pedant; and that the terms of the submission are to be found blended with the grand dogmas and high anticipations of the Advancement of Learning—this all who revere a great name must sorrowfully confess. That he suffered ample punishment for this offence and the other offences—into which he was betrayed less by an ambition for selfish honours than by a vain dream that they would reflect some dignity upon his studies and give some help in the pursuit of them,— ought to excuse us from passing any hard censure on his memory. But it could not rescue literature, in all its different forms, from a contraction, an impoverishment, which is all the more painful to remember when one considers the immense ability which was at work in every direction during James's reign, in verse and in prose, on the stage as well as in the pulpit. Unrivalled dramatic ability; but displayed in the representation of *humours*, not of *characters*; in the construction of most ingenious and impossible plots, not in illuminating history or common life; in exquisite conceits, often most musical songs, seldom in poetry that springs from the heart or goes to it. Whatever could be done in the way of elaborate composition, worthy to be admired for the study and diligence that were bestowed upon it, was done in that time. But the shadow of the king is over it all. We never can feel that we are out of the range of his influence; that his ingenious, coarse mind is not at work, spoiling the best thoughts, profaning the most sacred images. Our gratitude to Bacon must be all the greater for striking out a new path, in which these arts could be of no avail; for teaching men that it was more glorious to explore than to construct; for discovering the use of an instrument with which the king would not care to meddle, and which he could not turn aside by any exercise of his prerogative or his craft. Science might defy him; but till the appearance of the great Puritan poet in the next reign, literature had to endure patiently the gilded chains with which he had bound it.

In the great conflict between the king and the House of Commons, which lasted through the reigns of James and of his son, the bishops, as well as the men of letters, were inclined to regard that House as representing the Puritan feeling of the country in both its aspects—as hostile to the established ecclesiastical order, as hostile to the art and letters which the court patronised. There was an excuse for both opinions in that time; an excuse for their adoption by Mr. Gifford and many others, in a later time. Yet both opinions are extremely exaggerated; and, in the form in which they are often put, are contradicted by notorious facts. The Puritan party—that is to say, the party which regarded every approximation to Romanism with horror—was undoubtedly powerful among the freemen of the towns, as the Wyckliffite party had been in the Plantagenet period. Its strong convictions were fairly represented in the House of Commons, especially by those who sat for the towns. Among the freeholders there was, of course, less collision of opinion, more of the old traditions. Those who most truly represented their feelings were men strongly attached to the national order, opposed to Romanism, specially as interfering with *that*; but with no addiction to the special lessons of the Puritan preachers—averse from them so far as they were not national, so far as they tended to create any sect in the nation. These members of the House of Commons, so far from having any dislike to refined literature, were cultivated and travelled men, acquainted with the history and poetry of the old world, students of French and Italian history. The best and noblest specimen of the class is undoubtedly Sir John Eliot, whose sufferings had always made him a conspicuous figure in English history, and with whom we have become better acquainted lately through the valuable labours of Mr. Forster. It would be absurd to suppose that there were many of his stamp and calibre in either reign. But he was able to command the sympathies of a great many: they looked up to him as their leader. John Hampden, himself a country gentleman, was his intimate friend; there appears to have been the greatest fellowship of thought and sentiment between them. The question becomes a very interesting one, and one exceedingly important for the subject of these chapters—what it was that bound these men to the townspeople and their leaders, with whom they had so many real as well as apparent differences — what national feeling it was which the House of Commons embodied. The changes which that national feeling underwent may then be more easily explained; we may trace more clearly the connexion between the Stuart time and the Tudor time—between both these times and our own.

All readers of Clarendon will recollect the row of stately figures which he draws out before us at the commencement of his history. They represent the nobles who had survived the reign of James, and formed the court of his son. How dull and dreary and respectable they were, how utterly unaware that they were approaching a great crisis, how unprepared to meet it the writer makes us feel; he felt it himself. In the struggle that was at hand, it could not be predicted what part these noblemen would take; they might be swayed at times to either side; no distinct principle would determine their course; they had a sense of certain obligations to the order of the land, of certain others to the person of the monarch. Within these there was another circle; the favourite whom they had feared in the former reign, and who was master still; who had for a while been the popular champion while he opposed the Spanish alliance, but who was now regarded as the most mischievous of all the royal advisers, if he did not divide that fame, as well as his influence, with the queen. She—the centre of a much more graceful society than that of the previous reign, as she was the wife of a far more graceful man—had all the suspicion attaching to a French Roman Catholic, not untruly imagined to have a much stronger and steadier purpose than belonged to Charles. That he was quite free from his father's pedantry—that he admired the best painters, and bestowed favours on the most ingenious men, that the masques and entertainments which he patronised were such as any court might admire—so much all confess. But what was there in any literature which he cultivated that could raise or could reach the heart of a people? It helped those who had much time on their hands to kill it. Men who were full of fervour and earnestness found no nourishment in it; were repelled by it; could endure, if they did not love, the protests of such writers as Prynne against it.

The higher clergy approved these sports for the court; tolerated sports of another kind for the multitude. But what did they supply to those who were craving for illumination? They wrote tractates against Puritanism, they wrote tractates against Romanism. They promoted learning of a certain kind—useful antiquarian learning. Laud was very meritorious in this way. But such lore, desirable as it was, lay altogether out of the range of the people's thoughts—could have no influence upon them. The arguments against Romanism might be useful to persons in the court and the higher ranks who were inclined to that doctrine. The commons were not the least inclined to it. They suspected the sincerity of elaborate confutations which to them were unintelligible, and which appeared to have very slight effect upon those for whom they were intended. They did not suspect the sincerity of the attacks on Puritanism; by these they were irritated into increased sympathy with it. And the writings which were especially designed for their edification, which were to guide them out of the dangerous paths wherein they were wandering, were outrageous defences of the prerogative—violent attempts to wrest the Scriptures into witnesses that the sovereign was an irresponsible person—threats of what must follow if there were any questioning of his decrees.

Such writings were as utterly intolerable to the

educated gentlemen of England as they could be to the citizens. They felt that the king was putting forth his prerogative to the overthrow of the old laws and charters of the land. These were sacred witnesses in their eyes of the perpetuity of the nation; these were dear to all their family traditions and associations. The duty of adhering to these they learned from their classical instructors, as well as from the Jewish books. Tacitus told them what had come to Rome when the sense of law and the reverence for ancestors had been exchanged for subjection to the mere will of a man. The life and morals of a nation, they felt, were connected with the reverence for the past, with the belief in laws which no temporary decrees could set aside. Was not the court showing indifference to ancient forms and indifference to morality at the same time? Did it not palter with truth? Did it not depart from the word once given in a way that no English gentleman could bear to trifle with any word which had once gone out of his lips? And what were the clerical defences, but apologies in the name of God for insincerity, for falsehood? Could those be religious arguments against which the conscience protested? Did not they involve the sins which had been imputed to Jesuits? Must not they spring from the same principle? Must not they lead to the same result?

There was no Puritanism in such reflections as these. They belonged to the Englishman trained in the ordinary belief of his forefathers; instructed to worship a God of truth, and count all untruth the greatest abomination. But at this point they come into contact with the thoughts which the English citizen had received from the divines to whom he listened with the greatest sympathy; those who taught him to abhor every rag of idolatry, the slightest contact with the unclean thing; those who bade him count a Papist from Rome, or an Arminian from Amsterdam, as one carrying about with him the scent of the infernal pit. Such words could not have much influence on men who had visited Rome and Amsterdam, who had shared the hospitality of both Papists and Arminians. Yet it had in this application a very real significance for them also. That which threatened the subversion of their country's liberty, that which undermined their country's honesty, smelt as foully in their nostrils as it could in those of any Puritan. They were sure that it must be odious to Him who hates robbery for burnt-offering.

Here, then, would be a sufficient explanation of the fact that these two classes of men sat, as we should say in the dialect of our day, on the same side of the House, and joined in the same votes and denunciations. For a long time, what I may call the country-gentleman feeling appears to have the preponderance. The cry that charters should not be trampled upon, that the precedents of other days should be reverenced, that the king should not injure the honour of his throne by listening to mad and evil counsellors—these rose above all others. The ecclesiastics were included among the evil counsellors. If the dislike to them was sometimes greater than to any others, it was because the scandal of their support to the immoral acts of such men as Buckingham was intolerable to the English conscience; and because divines like Sibthorpe and Mainwaring were using the Book which Englishmen had accepted as the charter of their freedom to make them content with slavery.

In the first two Parliaments of Charles, Puritanism is chiefly seen co-operating with this national temper, which, in itself, is distinctly *not* Puritan. A change, I think, is manifest in the third Parliament. Such men as Pym, who represented the civic feeling, rose in influence; Eliot, of the other class, accepted, to a considerable extent, their maxims and watchwords. Had he ever left his prison and entered the House which assembled when parliaments came into existence again, he might have been obliged to accept them altogether.

Many have lamented this victory of the Puritan or civic party over that which was once rightly regarded as the country party. They have said that if the latter could have maintained its ground, the monarchy might have been reconciled with the House of Commons; there need have been no civil war, no protectorate. I cannot understand such speculations more than those about the Reformation, which might have been managed by Wolsey or Sir Thomas More.

I cannot imagine how the civil war or the protectorate could have been spared. I cannot cast the horoscope of England without them. I confess to a sympathy with such men as Eliot, which I cannot always feel for those who adopted the dialect of Puritanism. I confess that the civil war did become a religious war, and that the protectorate was the attempt to set up a kingdom of God in place of the Stuart kingdom, which had been put down. But it seems to me that the conflict for English freedom—that in which the English House of Commons engaged at this time—would have been a far more imperfect conflict than it was—would have left far less precious legacies behind it—if the element which the Puritan contributed to it had not proved itself to be the vital, and for a while the overpowering, one. What was grotesque, narrow, unreal in that element would be made more manifest through its success than it could be in any other way.

It seems to me that the claim of the king to such a divine delegation as gave him a right practically to do what he liked, could not be resisted by any reference to constitutional maxims—venerable and sacred as those maxims are. The most conspicuous members of the House of Commons—men not of a tender southern nature, but hard, tough, undemonstrative Englishmen, ashamed of betraying their feelings—actually burst into tears, we are told, on the great day of remonstrance, when the king trafficked with words in a double sense, and they felt that they must put themselves in direct opposition to him. No mere notion that legal forms or precedents were violated could have called forth such a passion as that. There was the under-conviction, that the king, in setting aside the old order, in trifling with the sincerity of human speech, was declaring war with a greater King; that the question was carried into a higher court; that the realm of England had subsisted from generation to generation under that sovereignty which Charles supposed had been transferred to him and was vested for the government of England at least in him.

Such a belief could not find full expression at once. But the strength of it became apparent, I am convinced, to at least one man. Thomas Wentworth, who had despised the court as long as Buckingham ruled it, who had used the same constitutional language which the other patriots used against the court, hated the Puritans more than he hated any counsellor of Charles. The moment it seemed to him that they were getting the ascendency, patriotism became disgusting to him. The constitutional forms might be worth something at other times. Let them be spurned, trodden under foot, placed at the mercy of an army, which he would gather together, rather than that the party to which Pym was attached should prevail. So I explain the conduct which his old friends regarded as a desertion, his close alliance with a man so unlike him as Laud, his desire that the king should reign without a Parliament, his readiness to stake his head on the success of his "thorough." The struggle, he perceived, was was no longer between different orders in the state. A belief which he connected with everything vulgar and enthusiastic must have the mastery, if he could not crush it with his Irish army. What signified all other considerations if this was the issue? Laud's dogmas and formalities might be insignificant and unintelligible in his eyes; but they were the only spiritual agency that he knew which could be set against the Puritan agency. Laud was evidently as much in earnest as he was, as ready to destroy or to die rather than succumb to his foes. This was a bond of fellowship between them. Let him set up Episcopacy in Scotland with what weapons he could, Strafford would try to forge others, that were, in his judgment, much more efficient weapons.

The Scotch scheme was disappointed. The Covenant came forth in its strength. The name of God was invoked against the name of the king. The Scotch nation bowed to it, the English army retreated, the Long Parliament was summoned. The most courageous of its opponents were the first whom it grappled with. Nothing could be done till Strafford was taken out of the way. The court gave up the man whose purposes had always been too distinct and vast for it. But Laud also was impeached. The seats of the bishops in the House of Lords were at once threatened. The House of Commons decreed its own perpetuity. It was evident that the forms of the constitution were not henceforth to be the motives of the conflict. Yet it must be remembered that some of those who adhered to those forms most tenaciously—who ultimately fought for the king when they supposed that the Parliament was violating them—assented to some of the strongest of these measures. Falkland spoke and voted for the motion to deprive the bishops of their seats. Their defences of the prerogative, he evidently felt, had deluded the king into his worst measures and had undermined the order of the commonwealth. Hyde dissented from his friend on this subject, though in general they were in agreement as to the mischief of the course into which Charles had gone. Soon they both became his advisers, so far as the queen would permit them; for they believed that the watchword of the Covenant must become the watchword of the Parliamentary leaders, however they might seek for some other. At the beginning of the war it appeared as if some other had been found. Essex and Manchester had no interest in supporting Presbyterianism against Episcopacy—and was not that what the Covenant meant? Their cause, they said, was the cause of the old order of the kingdom, yes, of the king himself against his evil advisers. But how languidly they fought with such names as these on their banners! Who cared to follow them? The better men in the royal army had the old love for the person of the king. Some, like Falkland, felt that their cause was now that of law as well as of king. The worst of them had the hatred of Puritanism and the love of wine and wassail to give them zeal. What inspiration was there in the Parliamentary army to meet this? But might not some in those armies really care that Presbyterianism should conquer Episcopacy? No doubt some London apprentices did care; their preachers told them that it was an object worth caring for. There was one in the army of Fairfax who listened patiently to such admonitions, and on whom they produced exceedingly slight effect. Systems of church government were as little to Cromwell as Parliamentary formulas. He did not believe in one more than in the other. Nor did he trust the London apprentices, or the preachers, much more than the aristocratical generals, to secure the triumph of the cause to which he was devoted. The Scotch Covenant meant to him the setting up of the name of God against the name of the earthly king, not at all the setting up of Presbyterianism against Episcopacy. The soldiers whom he gathered about him had no Scotch feeling. They were altogether English—of the class of freeholders, I apprehend, rather than of freemen; brought from the country for the most part, though no doubt with a fair sprinkling of the citizens, provided they would submit to drill and learn obediently how to use their arms. At first it may not have been perceived that the Ironsides were working that double change of which I have spoken. It may have been fancied that they only threw the aristocratical leaders into the background, and that they would gladly allow the Westminster Assembly to utter its decrees and organise the land according to its system; the new soldiers would put down their enemies and establish their authority. The new soldiers had no such dream; their leader was as free from it as they were. Baxter found, when he mixed with them as a chaplain, that they understood none of his distinctions, that they could not appreciate his moderation. If the distinctions did not mean that there was a divine kingdom which their swords were to establish, what were they good for? If his moderation was to hinder them in that work, must he not be one of the wicked? What inspiration had he which was not equally theirs? "Yes," their chief would have told them, "you are quite right, my friends, you have this inspiration, and you are to use it for this end. But if it interferes with discipline, if it prevents you from obeying orders, it is evil inspiration, and I must put it down." And what he said must be done, he always did.

It is easy to talk of the enthusiasm of Cromwell and his troops, and of the victory which that enthusiasm won. But the enthusiasm, I suspect, had a ground and an object, or it could not have prevailed; all the less if there was mixed with it, as we think there was, so much of what was weak and fantastic. The ground and the object had been con-

tinually proclaimed in creeds and acts of worship by
their opponents; the Ironsides did not assert the
dominion of God, or His influence over the hearts
and spirits of men, more strongly than it had been
asserted by those who called them fanatics and
rebels. But it had been asserted without being
believed. It had passed into a phrase, a mere " term
of art," to use an expression of Jeremy Taylor's.
When it presented itself to the minds of English
freeholders and freemen as a truth—a truth which
was the foundation of all their liberty, and yet which
had been twisted into a proof that they were not free
—the consequences which followed are not astonishing. The trial of the king, who had fallen into their
hands and about whom there had been so many
insincere negotiations, may appear to us one of the
greatest outrages upon justice and order. It appeared so to a great part of the land, to the Presbyterians as well as the Episcopalians. But to men
become suddenly possessed of *this* conviction, it appeared like the vindication of an order and justice
which had been set at nought—like a sentence coming forth from the highest Throne against an earthly
throne which had lifted itself up against that. Whatever perversion there was in the feeling—however
righteous our protest against the result to which it
led—we gain nothing by confounding it with an
entirely different feeling, defended upon entirely
different maxims, which was at work a century and
a half later in France. We gain nothing; we lose

much for the understanding of that period, and of all subsequent periods in our history.

The purging of the House of Commons, the closing of the House of Lords, before the death of the king, show clearly enough that a dislike of monarchy and a preference for the other branches of the constitution had nothing to do with this act. A love for the rule of the House of Commons was certainly no part of Cromwell's creed now. I do not see how it can ever have held any strong place in his mind. The Long Parliament, he thought, had been called to do a work. When the king was dead, when his son was subdued, had it any more work to do? It had said that it was immortal. Could it really make itself immortal? Did it any longer represent the freemen of the towns or the freeholders of the country? They seemed not to think that it did; to be rather weary of it. But some one was wanted to say that they were weary of it. If Cromwell undertook the office, it was not an exception from his other acts. It was exactly in the spirit of them. He could not dissolve the Parliament; but he could say, "Go your ways, the nation does not need you longer; the Lord of all does not need you longer."

That was the end of the House of Commons which had exalted itself so high; which had done much for the land; which was striving to make itself the one estate of the realm. It could not be that. Cromwell spoke the language of fact, of reason, even of old constitutional maxims, though he might not care

THE CALL TO RULE. 121

much for them, when he said that it could not. There must be some one to convoke a Parliament. It must sit to advise one who administered, not to administer itself. The notion of its electing such a one, or of the body of the people electing such a one, would have clashed as much with the ideas of Cromwell as with those of any Stuart. He, more than any Stuart, believed that the chief ruler must have a divine call to his office, in whatever way he is made aware of it. And he did not conceive, so far as one can judge from his acts, that he had the least call to be an unchecked ruler—a ruler without a council. He tried to get parliaments—I think, to get them fairly chosen; though he may not have succeeded well in his experiment. The longer he held his office, the less he showed a wish to make it dependent on the pleasure of the army, the more he strove to connect it with such institutions as the country had known and recognised. It must depend upon our estimate of his character, whether we judge him to be sincere in these endeavours, and sincere also in his hesitation about the crown. I take him to have been sincere in both; to have had a sense that his position was given him, and that he must not part with it; to have felt that it would be a truer position, if it were not at variance with the ancient order of things; and, at the same time, that there was the danger of making a childish imitation of the old order; that it was a folly to clothe himself with a name which was surrounded with hereditary associations, and had scarcely any meaning apart from them. To the worth of such associations he bore witness to the last, and what we may regard in one aspect of it as the strangest act of his life, his nomination of Richard to be his successor. Monstrous as the contradiction was of appointing a man without the least sign or dream of a calling to a function which he exercised solely in the faith that he possessed one, yet the contradiction was a homage to a principle that he had seemed to set at naught. After that acknowledgment, the restoration of Prince Charles was clearly inevitable. The English people may not be as logical as some others; but they have a certain sense of moral consistency which sometimes supplies the place of logic.

Any one who contemplates this series of events, may feel exceeding gratitude to Mr. Carlyle for scattering some of the mists in which court, clerical, constitutional, and republican historians had enveloped the life of Cromwell. It is not the exaggeration of a hero-worshipper to say that Cromwell interprets the Puritan movement of the time, redeems it from its merely sectarian character, shows it to have had a might which the preachers could not have imparted to it, and which no parliamentary government could express. The exaggeration of the hero-worshipper only appears when the man is glorified to the denial of the very truth which the man asserted; when the belief in a divine government, permanent through all changes of outward events, is treated as having perished with him, and as needing the avatar of some similar champion to restore it. Supposing he was right—supposing what he said, and strove, amidst strange confusions, to translate into action, was not a phantasy,—it ought to be good for all the previous and for all the subsequent stages of English history. An interruption in the sequence of that history must then have been permitted, not really to break the chain of it, but to show how closely all the links of it are bound together; to explain what truth was hidden under the arbitrary claims of monarchs, under the ambition of churchmen, as well as under all the protests against those arbitrary claims and that ambition; to discover the great worth of a representative assembly, as well as the limits of its worth; to give us some scale for ascertaining the power of a religious conviction in promoting moral and political freedom; some test of the check which the same conviction imposes on moral and political freedom, when it loses its life and passes into the symbol of a smaller or a larger, a patronised or a militant school.

On all these subjects the life and writings of Milton are even a clearer commentary than the acts of the Protector whom he served. The student of English history during the first sixty years of the seventeenth century should never try to spell out the hieroglyphics which he will find in it, without the use of this cipher, as well as of the other. There is no part of Milton's beautiful career which does not contribute something to our illumination. The boy who came from the scrivener's house in Cheapside—from the Puritan lessons of his father and mother—to spend his nights and days at St. Paul's school in imbibing the old heathen wisdom—already foretold how the Hebrew lore was to sustain and quicken the Greek lore in his mind, till they found their full and final union in the choruses which sang how the blinded and down-trodden Israelite should yet see his enemy at his feet. It was even a rarer gift to combine a devoted study of the old romances with the continual growth of manliness and purity of heart; a delight in every sight and sound of the outward world, with a profound awe of the eye and voice of the secret Taskmaster; the enjoyment of the cloister and the cathedral, with the anticipation of the two-handed engine at the door, which stood ready to smite once, and smite no more; a vigorous, even prudent Protestantism, with such an enjoyment of the literature, the language, the friendship of Italians as they had supposed that no northern could possess. Then came the glorious day when the Long Parliament was summoned. To witness the reformation which it was to introduce, what bright visions in Italy and Greece must not be left behind! What weary toil with untractable schoolboys in Aldersgate Street may not be endured! For now ecclesiastical tyranny is to be scattered, the poor Presbyter is to put down the proud prelate! Yes, the day of the House of Commons is indeed a day of the Lord! Alas! we must yet hear of forcers of conscience in this very Parliament; we must discover that new Presbyter is but old priest writ large. The poet must stand before the House of Commons of England to plead against their purpose of strangling at birth the sacred progeny of men's brains; to ask that the assertors of freedom would not bind the press with new chains forged by themselves. The disappointment is very grievous; yet still he holds right onward, bating not a jot of heart or hope. The king's death is for him the vindication of that divine right which had been converted into a plea for mortal prerogative. He can bear the loss of the assembly which once seemed to promise all blessing, for

> "Cromwell, our chief of men, that through a cloud,
> Not of war only, but distractions rude,
> Guided by faith and matchless fortitude,
> To peace and truth his glorious way has plough'd,"

might yet

> "Help us to save free conscience from the paw
> Of hireling wolves, whose gospel is their maw."

A pursuit of freedom surely for many a weary hour; through all changes of times and circumstances, through all failures of human agents. A pursuit which must seem to many a profitless endeavour. Milton knew that it was not so. He knew that freedom did not depend, never had depended, upon these human agents. Every step in his painful discoveries had led him more to see that it belongs to the spirit of man; that parliaments and protectors can give it as little as kings—preachers as little as prelates; that all may do something to crush or weaken the hearts in which it should dwell and grow ; that all may do something to strengthen it in those hearts, if they will confess a God who demands obedience of his creatures as the condition of their freedom.

The sense of this union was never so strong in Milton as in those evil days on which he complained that he had fallen. The men who were flushed with insolence and wine showed him how indifference to the one involved the loss of the other. " Paradise Lost" and " Paradise Regained" embodied his conception of their separation and of their reconciliation. There is the greatest possible contrast between the lofty and various music of a poem and the vulgar actualities of a colonial existence ; yet it seems to me sometimes as if New England were a translation into prose of the thought that was working in Milton's mind from its early morning to its sunset.

And what was to become, in those days which appeared to him so evil, and which in many respects were so evil, of the House which he had once hoped would work deliverance for the nation ? Let us not suppose that the Restoration brought back all which the civil wars had taken away. The abolition of the tenure of knight-service by one of the early acts of Charles II.'s reign may have affected chiefly the greater landed proprietors. It was, however, the recognition of a change which was going on through the whole land; it was a sign that feudalism had done its work, and was in process of dissolution. The civil wars had produced an effect similar to that of the wars of the Roses. What the first Tudor king had done from policy and necessity combined, the restored Stuart king assented to from necessity simply. He was too indolent to have a policy. But feudalism had been among the traditions of his house; his father had lamented the weakening of it as one of the causes of his own failure. I am far from considering that weakness, now more than in the time of Henry VII., as an unmixed blessing. The money power now, as then, was threatening to be in the ascendant. There was much in the temper of the restoration age which led to the belief in it as the great power of the universe. But there were some of the circumstances of the time, even of its calamitous circumstances, which tended to check this danger in a class that was most likely to be affected by it. The citizens of the towns had always been in danger of magnifying personal wealth, as the gentry were in danger of magnifying landed wealth. The Wyckliffite influence had been their protector from this danger in the earlier times. The reverence which they felt for the Nonconformist preachers who resigned their livings at the passing of the Act of Uniformity, was a counteraction to it at this time. The creation of such a body of separatists was, of course, an enormous evil. The persecutions which were inflicted upon them constituted one of the great crimes of the civil and ecclesiastical rulers of Charles's reign. But both one and the other had this attendant blessing—they gave the citizens a set of teachers who had a moral influence over them—a more direct access to their minds than those would have had who used the Prayer-book. And the sufferings of these men awakened in the trading class a belief in qualities which they would not otherwise have recognised, a respect for the want of the gold which it was the temptation to idolise.

When we are casting up the accounts of this time, these items must always enter into the calculation. The notorious corruptions and profligacy of the court must not usurp all our notice. A strange fermentation was going on in the land, of which that profligacy was one symptom, and of which there were other symptoms scarcely less melancholy. But if we look below the surface, we shall discover proofs that the nation was shaping itself into a kind of order, and that the influences which most contributed to its disorder might ultimately be brought into harmony.

On the whole, I believe the House of Commons throughout this reign was a fair index of its character, a true representation of that which was working in it both for destruction and towards health. As an institution it has established its place. The notion of doing without it has passed out of the Stuart mind. Its power may be often inconvenient, but it must be recognised. When we look into it, we see that two parties have formed themselves in it, very like and very unlike the old Cavaliers and Roundheads. The

Tories and Whigs seem exactly to correspond to these. They are their legitimate successors. Nothing is wanting to each but the *faith* which was found in the former time. The Tory does not really see any divinity in the person of the king, though he has a theory which assumes that a divinity does of right belong to him. The Whig is inclined to smile at the acknowledgment of a divine ruler of the nation which was contained in the Covenant, though he has derived his nickname from those who followed Argyle, and who would have died for the Covenant. An immense transformation, no doubt—connected with the vehement reaction of this period, with disgust for the cant phrases of the former period, with the desire if possible to separate its politics from any associations with them. But this proves to be absolutely impossible. Every measure which is introduced into the House brings back the ideas to which these phrases pointed, associates them with patent facts or terrible fears. The House is occupied with trying to put down conventicles, or with arresting popish plots, or with excluding the Duke of York lest he should introduce popery. The old names cannot be got rid of, the old impressions cannot be got rid of. In this indevout time there are more phantasms, more monstrous impostures, all coming forth under religious names and appealing to religious fears and suspicions, than were ever heard of in the parliament of Barebones. Foreign affairs are as much under this influence as home affairs. Louis XIV. may have wondered to think what different questions stirred the English nation from those which had occupied France in the days of the Fronde. But he found that these were the questions which interfered with his ascendency in the councils of England; that it was not difficult to have kings for his pensioners; but that he must make the kings independent of their parliaments, he must profit by their preference for the religion of a gentleman—if he was to effect his object of reducing England into a province of the great monarchy.

The House of Commons, therefore, whilst it reflected the turmoil, the scepticism, the fanaticism of the land, was really its preserver. The weakening of its power through the wild counsels into which it was led, was the cause of the triumph of the Court at the end of the reign and of the reckless use which it made of that triumph. Reckless in one sense, but not inconsiderate. In taking away the charters from the towns, the Court was striking at one of its greatest enemies, one of the powers which had been a chief restraint upon absolutism. To undermine municipal government was the most natural, the most reasonable road to arbitrary rule.

The reign of James II. ratified all these lessons, and brought them to their climax. It was felt to be more and more impossible to sever the questions which involved faith from those which concerned government. Every step in the career of James brought them into closer fellowship, compelled the statesmen to recognise their combination, however little they might feel disposed to fall back upon the language or the notions of the Cromwell period. The acts of James had a corresponding effect upon the different religious parties, upon Conformists and upon Nonconformists equally. The bishops had preached passive obedience; the Nonconformists were beginning to content themselves with authority over their congregations, to give up the dream of influencing the government of states. Both were compelled to change their course; the former certainly with the most awkwardness. The common enemy brought them together; the Dissenters became the defenders of the bishops, the bishops became the victims of the king. There was a strange dance of parties, a curious interlacing of interests; what was more consolatory, a confession of principle, a submission to duty in opposing parties. But for this the Revolution could never have taken place. For so all mere notions about the divine authority of kings, all mere notions about the separation of religious questions from political questions, all mere notions about the crime of resistance or the right of resistance, gave way to the belief—diffused wonderfully through all classes of the land—that there is a will which is higher than that of any mortal or any dynasty, and that there are moments when it is treason against this higher will not to treat the authority of the lower as abrogated. The coming of William to our shores brought this belief into definite action; Somers, and those who framed the Declaration of Rights, gave it a formal expression in words.

I hold this Declaration to be a ratification of the Puritan principle, of the real doctrine which had been asserted in the Scotch Covenant, stripped of all sectarian technicalities, and identified with the old principles of the constitution. In this sense I cannot think that its worth has been the least overrated by the Whig historians, though they have, in their eagerness to clear themselves of all fellowship with their godly predecessors, explained away unfairly the language of the Declaration—reading it by the light of Locke's defence of what he took to be its principles in his "Essay on Governments." I do not undervalue that masterly work if I prefer to read a document of such grandeur and significance by its own light and by the light of all the previous history of our land.

I cannot think that the events of William's reign, and, above all, the doings of its Parliaments, offer us any encouragement to accept a party view of the transactions with which it commenced. The parties of the time—let who will represent them to us— come forth with anything but brilliancy and honour. If Lord Macaulay is the Whig historian, he has certainly done little to make us in love with his own school, though we may admire their opponents even less. He is probably right in his main conception— into whatever occasional idolatries and concealment of dark spots in his favourite character it may have betrayed him—that the king was the great preserver of the land, that he prevented the rival parties from destroying it. Such a proof of the worth of monarchy was exceedingly important at a time when so many influences had tended to bring it into disesteem, when the Revolution itself might have suggested the idea that the representative House was the supreme authority. All the events of this time as much confute that doctrine as they establish the dignity of the House, whilst it preserves its true character and office. It was passing, in the reign of William III., into a new phase. It was as much on its trial as it ever has been in any later period. A very severe trial indeed, it was; one not to ascertain its functions, but to see how it would use them when they had been fully conceded and defined. I will not anticipate the result; I will only make two observations upon the period which has been under our review.

The first has reference to the whole of it. The people, I think it is evident, have been growing during the century between the reign of James I. and the reign of Anne—growing, to use the distinction of Laertes, in thews and outward bulk—growing in the inward service of the mind and will. The growth has an outward development: serfs emancipated, freemen and freeholders multiplied; the House which they call theirs, taking up a magnificent position as defenders of freedom; then claiming an authority which was incompatible with freedom; straining its cords till they burst; finally, becoming the genuine expression of whatever there was in the mind of the country to express, its wisdom or its folly, its belief and unbelief, its unity and its factions. The people, now as before, is not identical with the Commons. The Commons cannot assume to be the people, without weakening themselves. But in them lies the developing power of the people. What they are determines what it shall be.

The next remark has especial reference to those last reigns of which I have been speaking. To understand them, we must observe not merely the outward condition of the time, but all that gives us a clue as to its education, its secret life. I have referred often to the literature of this period. I have taken Milton as the highest specimen and illustration of the century down to the Restoration. I do not think you can find a better illustration of the period subsequent to it than Dryden. The contrast between the two men, between the styles and subjects of their poems and of their prose, is, in fact, the contrast between the periods in which they flourished. A most pathetic history of a man and of an age is that which we read when we begin from Dryden's "Monody on the Death of Cromwell;" when we go on to the "Astræa Redux," which commemorates the glories of the Restoration; when we study his Ahithophel; when we pass from his "Religion of a Layman," wherein he performs the part of an Anglican advocate, to the "Hind and Panther," wherein he defends Romanism. The political vicissitudes in the two first poems—the manifestation of all the party feeling and personal grudges of the time in the satire on Shaftesbury and Monmouth —the exhibition of the two last poems—a faithful exhibition, as I think—of the way in which a most accomplished man, not governed by any moral conviction or principle, adopts a religious system, and maintains it with much learning and very ingenious arguments, then drifts into another which offers him the promise of greater repose — these are such pictures of a generation as only a great artist, and an artist who was drawing from the world within, as much as from the world without, could have bequeathed to us. These changes were imaged, as I take it, in the House of Commons. Was there nothing permanent also which was imaged in it? We have seen the patriots in the reign of Charles I. claiming it to be the witness for abiding forms of the constitution. We have seen it surviving a civil war, coming out, after a revolution in which Dryden saw only the triumph of a Dutch stadtholder, fresh and vigorous. It is not the institution which is inconstant. The inconstancy is in those whom the institution represents. If they have any stability in them—any feeling of fellowship with the past and the future, it will not fail to stamp itself upon those whom they send forth to speak in their name. Clearly mere attachment to an old family —mere dislike of Puritans and Whigs— does not confer that stability. Dryden had these, and he is the very type of the mutability of his time.

CHAPTER V.

THE HOUSE OF COMMONS IN THE EIGHTEENTH CENTURY.

I HAVE endeavoured to show that the phrase "Representative System," if it is derived from the circumstances of one Assembly, is an inadequate or misleading one. The Commons are represented, or ought to be, in the Commons' House. The monarch is also represented. The ministers, what we call the Cabinet, represent the sovereign to his subjects, as much as those who are elected by boroughs or counties represent the subjects to the sovereign.

It has not been necessary to dwell much on *this* representation in the periods through which we have travelled. The king we have found occupying a very substantial position, exercising a very direct influence on the country which he ruled. Shakespeare felt that all our history was the history of reigns; the monarch was practically, not nominally, the centre of its movements. I observed that he had brought this maxim to the severest test. Richard II., utterly feeble and self-indulgent, must still be the leading person of his drama. Henry VI., longing to change the sceptre for the shepherd's crook, and justifying his desire by his acts, still is our guide through the distractions of the civil war; his wife, every one of his nobles, may have a greater mental or physical force than he has; yet he interprets their acts to us; he is the one peaceful figure in the hurly-burly, saving it from being a pure anarchy.

This conception of past history was abundantly justified, as I observed, by Shakespeare's Tudor experience. I did not deny that the next age was one from which he could not have learnt the lesson. James I., assuming to be more a king than all his predecessors, was essentially less of one; he had many gifts; the specially kingly gifts seemed to have been carefully withholden from him. It was in his reign and in the next reign, that the distinction between the person of the king and his evil counsellors began to be dwelt upon with especial emphasis; it became the characteristic phraseology of the first three parliaments of Charles; it was not dropped by the Long Parliament; it was preserved through the earlier years of the war. The distinction seems often most difficult to maintain—yet it had expressed at first the sincere loyalty of those who used it; afterwards their *desire* to be loyal. When they began to suspect that it was a fiction, the struggle in the conscience of the nation was fearful. It issued in the death of the king. He could not be separated from his advisers. He must have been the source of their evil acts. He must be more guilty than they were. Only a few could adopt that terrible logic. There was a revolt against it in the people generally. The restored king was welcomed with passionate affection. There was a determination not to see wrong in him, whatever wrongs he might do. He tempted that resolution fearfully. Suspected Romanism—suspected transactions with the French king; these belonged to him individually: they could not be transferred to his advisers. Still he was forgiven for his good-nature. His subjects acquired so much of his image that they could not dislike him. James was evidently independent of his counsellors; he followed out his own personal tastes and persuasions; he braved the responsibility of them, and fell. His successor had recognised advisers—sometimes Whig, sometimes Tory; but the management of European policy which interested him most, he took upon himself. He was, as Lord Macaulay is careful to point out, his own minister for foreign affairs. Up to the close of the seventeenth century, then, this representation of the monarch by ministers has not been prominent. It has suggested itself often; it has not forced itself upon us as a cardinal fact of the history.

This it becomes in the eighteenth century. It not only cannot be overlooked; no political facts can be contemplated apart from it. All questions respecting the House of Commons can only be viewed in relation to it. The character and influence of that House are determined, in a great measure, by it. There are, in fact, for our purpose but three great topics to be considered in the life of the eighteenth century. First, how this representation of the sovereign by ministers affected the education and representation of the people; secondly, how this education and representation were influenced by certain great *material* changes which took place in the condition of England; thirdly, how they were affected by certain *moral* movements which occurred here, and by certain others, apparently of a very different character, which took place in France in the course of this century.

1. How the notion of the divine right *in* the sovereign had influenced the minds of the Stuart princes—how it had been encountered by the strong Puritan belief of a divine right *over* the sovereign—we have seen. That struggle is, in fact, the history of the seventeenth century. It had terminated; but it had left its legacies. The belief in a divine right had passed into the most elaborate and artificial scheme about the way in which this divine right had been obtained. Adam had received it by a special grant from God; he had transmitted it, through various channels, to different patriarchal monarchs; somehow it had descended, or a portion of it had descended, upon the kings of England. How could such an authority, dating from the very day of creation, be set aside by any presumptuous people in the seventeenth century after Christ?

Such was the doctrine of Sir R. Filmer, which

must have had considerable hold on the public mind, or on something which called itself the public mind, since Locke did not scorn to refute it in his " Essay on Government." How easily hands skilful as his were could tear such a web as this to pieces, need not be told; if demolition was needed, the demolition was perfect. But if this was the best embodiment of his thought which the Tory could invent, surely the Whig might have a much, better. Locke undertook to provide him with one. There was no descent of authority from Adam upon a race of monarchs; but there was, at some time or other, somewhere or other, a contract entered into between a society and the man or men by whom it pleased to be governed. So long as the contract was observed, there could be no wish in the subjects to get rid of their rulers. It might be broken, and then they were quite justified in doing what England had done in the case of James II.

The accomplished statesmen in the reign of Queen Anne, who adopted the Tory side, had as little belief as possible in the dogmas of Sir Robert Filmer. It was convenient for the clergy to be provided with such arguments. The pulpits would send them forth. They would have an influence on the vulgar. They would help the statesmen in pursuing their scheme of policy at home or abroad. The statesmen would, of course, be bound to reward the Churchmen for their aid, by assisting them against the Dissenters. They would also defend the landed interest, their natural allies, against the city or moneyed interest, which always inclined to their opponents. If they did not directly support the exiled family, they could comfort the queen with the assurance that she had as good a divine right as her father or grandfather. Such were nearly the maxims of St. John—the most sagacious of the champions of the Tory and High Church party—the most utter disbeliever in all which priests of one communion or another taught then, or ever had taught.

Was the faith of Sir Robert Walpole, the leading Whig of that reign and of the succeeding reign, in the doctrine of a contract, much deeper or firmer than that of St. John in Sir Robert Filmer? One faith, I conceive, answered very fairly to the other. It was exceedingly well for philosophers, if they liked, to have a well-compacted theory. It was useful for those who were writing pamphlets against the Tories to be furnished with an available argument. But statesmen had business on their hands which left them no leisure for such questions. They were to hold things together as well as they could, whilst they were in office, to show cause against their opponents whilst they were out of it. As for notions about the origin of government—well, those who could believe in them, might do so.

I have taken my specimens not only from the two opposite schools, but from the two typical men of these schools—men personally as well as politically hostile to each other, men most unlike in all the habits of their minds; the one ostentatiously a philosopher and man of letters, the other ostentatiously a man of business who despised philosophy and letters. But the result is the same in both cases. A fiction is supposed to underlie the whole of society. The sovereign himself is that fiction. To the Tory statesman as to the Whig, he becomes merely an ornamental appendage to the system of government. The party which predominates in the House of Commons, and out of which the Cabinet is chosen, these constitute the government. The sovereign is their puppet; what he is signifies little, only what they can make him do by moving their wires.

There were many signs during the eighteenth century that the supposed puppet could exhibit an inconvenient vitality and energy. Queen Anne, swayed by her Duchess of Marlborough and her Mrs. Masham, could show her masters that their places depended on her favour. George I. and George II. were continually disturbing the purposes of the ministers by their determination to protect their own electoral dominions, and to use the arms of England for their support. George III. would have established independence of his ministers into a maxim of his government. All these proceedings, however, being fruits of self-will, and evidently injurious to the land, only seemed to support the notion that it was desirable as much as possible to limit the action of the sovereign, to reduce him into a cipher.

But if politicians can easily persuade themselves

to accept a fiction, a nation cannot. It must have a faith: and the faith must be in a person, not in a notion or a congeries of notions. The English people no more regarded the sovereign as a cipher now than in former days. There was not much in Queen Anne to inspire reverence. But they recognised her as a British princess; something of the tenderness and chivalry which female sovereigns always have called forth, was directed towards her as it had been towards her sister. Loyalty might be a harder task towards Germans who could not speak our language, who did not understand our customs, who imported some that were very offensive. But to zealous Protestants, to those who dreaded arbitrary rule, they represented a principle. They represented it; the principle without them would have been an abstraction; so they drew a kind of affection towards them, which their disagreeable acts and qualities could not extinguish. George III. as a Briton born, received at his accession much of the loyalty which had been bestowed on the Stuart over the water; that which had been withdrawn from his predecessors. He alienated the Whigs, insulted the most popular of all ministers, created a strong suspicion that his British birth had not preserved him from the maxims of his mother, which were not British at all. But again and again, the affection which he had first enkindled, revived; his prejudices often helped it to procure it for him; his calamity riveted it. Never had the monarchy endured ruder shocks than during these reigns;

never was it more proved to be a reality, possessing the greatest influence for good and evil, apart from those representatives in whom it was supposed to be swallowed up, as well as through them. For these representatives could not separate their existence from the sovereign. The people understood them to be what they were called, his servants; the notion that they were his substitutes would have destroyed their power.

There was, however, this curious contradiction, which has often been noticed as specially characteristic of the first two reigns of the House of Brunswick. The Tories, whose creed seemed to consist in attachment to the person of the monarch, only submitted with sullenness to the rule of German princes; the Whigs, whose creed was to reverence institutions above persons, were continually tempted to trifle with the institutions of the country for the sake of maintaining the existing family on the throne. It was this perplexity of parties, this uncertainty whether either of them meant what it said, or knew what it meant, which makes us feel that the House of Commons during the first half of this century had lost all the greatness which belonged to it in the former century. What, we ask, did it express? Some conviction, doubtless, there was in its members; perhaps two opposite convictions, each important to the well-being of the land. But have they any force, any charm in them which can resist the vulgarest temptation? Sir Robert Walpole says not; he knows the price of every man. One hopes that he lied; such boasts have been made at other times in reference to other subjects, and we accept them as indications of the character of the speaker more than of those about whom he speaks. But that the words should have gone forth at all—that a prudent man should have counted it prudent to indulge in such a vaunt—even that it should have been attributed to him—is a sign that either by public auction or private contract the consciences of men in high stations were to be had, and that neither buyer nor seller was much ashamed of the transaction. To Sir Robert Walpole, I apprehend, who was far from a bad man, it appeared a quite inevitable arrangement. He saw no other way of keeping out the Pretender, and preserving the country in tolerable prosperity. If statesmen demanded bribes that they might do what seemed to him the best thing for the country, was he to refuse them? He must use the materials which he found. He had no call to make them better.

Such apologies would occur naturally to a man who probably was a more competent administrator than most of those who found fault with him. They indicated the victory of that great money power which had already shown itself in the South Sea speculation. They showed that there was no belief awake in the House of Commons, or in those who chose the members of it, which could successfully struggle with this money power. Some protests against it came from the Tory squires. They felt that the dignity of the land was at stake; that the fundholders were becoming an estate in the realm; that in a little time they might be supreme. Lord Bolingbroke hinted to them that Sir Robert Walpole was the agent of the fundholder; that they must collect their strength and be ready to part with old names and prejudices in their warfare against him. His letter to Sir William Wyndham on Parties is a highly interesting document, illustrating the action of a man of extraordinary ability and no real conviction upon the country gentleman class; his skilful management of their passions and partialities; his efforts to indoctrinate them with a political philosophy which is strange to them, that he may accomplish a personal object which they have in common; altogether showing how many fine things may be said without much principle to bind them together, but how little can be done until some man shall appear who in his heart despises dishonesty and corruption, who feels that he cannot faithfully represent either Commons or King unless he has a higher object than that of securing the favour of either.

It was the serious conviction of the English people that the elder Pitt was such a man. They might credit him with it before he deserved the reputation, whilst he was still mixed in the discreditable politics of the Prince of Wales, whilst he was dreaming that odious family feuds could promote the prosperity of a nation. But the instinct which raised him to be the great commoner, was a true instinct, one which has been recognised as true by historians of the most dissimilar tempers. He believed that there was something besides a voracious stomach in the House of Commons, and in the people generally; he spoke to a heart in them; and one came forth in answer to his speech. There was that in those very men whose price Walpole knew, which was not willing to sell itself, which could confess a higher standard than gold. The statesman who acted as if there was, could command a sympathy which Walpole had not been able to procure. And because he knew a good man, and could frown upon a bad, he was able to administer the affairs of the nation in the midst of a war which involved four continents, as Walpole, with all his skill, had not been able to administer them in the midst of peace.

The consequence was, that though Pitt belonged to no great Whig family, and was connected with no strong Whig traditions, he was able to maintain the old Whig principle, which gave so much dignity to the House of Commons as the organ of the country's voice, in a way which none of his predecessors had done. Walpole had made the House ignominious, whilst his maxim bound him to assert its importance. Pitt really vindicated its dignity by treating it as if it was an assembly of gentlemen, not of tradesmen who had come to find the best market for the most worthless of all commodities, themselves. He vindicated also the dignity of the Crown by bringing it into sympathy with the Commons. He restored the popularity of the occupier of the throne by showing that his German sympathies might be enlisted in support of a cause and a monarch that were dear to the nation.

The difference between that monarch and one who merely acted through representatives, or who was shackled by a parliament, has been vividly brought before us by Mr. Carlyle. Let his display of Frederick's power of judging and acting for himself have all the credit and worth that can be given it. But let us, also, not fail to observe that the honest historian has exhibited with all his own clearness and vigour, the terrible disasters which his hero suffered from refusing to be represented by his generals in great battles; from choosing, through an "Olympian temper," to interfere just at the moment when it was most important to trust them and let them determine for themselves. Nearly every defeat which threatened the existence of the Prussian kingdom was caused, if we accept Mr. Carlyle's narrative as true, by this kind of self-will. No book, therefore, suggests more directly than his the thought that there may be —nay, that there must be—some way of reconciling kingly strength and government with that apparent absorption of it into responsible ministers which appears to be implied in our Constitution, and to have been developed in the eighteenth century. In peace, just as much as in war, there may be a way of recognising his representatives, which takes nothing from the dignity, even from the free action, of the sovereign; which only proves his self-restraint, and preserves him from ignominious failures.

It will be admitted that the less there is of pettiness or pettishness in any ruler, the less he yields to any mere private fancies or influences, the more he fulfils his function. Suppose there were two principles really at work in the mind of the English nation at this time; two principles, with neither of which it could dispense, yet which could not be brought into fellowship; was the sovereign a puppet or a cipher, if, instead of merely following his own will, he expressed, in the choice of his ministers, the one which at a given time had obtained predominance,—he himself perpetually suggesting by the changes in his ministers, that there was somewhere a synthesis of these principles, however little he or any philosopher might be able to state it in formal words, however perilous might be the experiment of forcing either party to abandon its own maxims for the sake of giving effect to those of the other? That there were two such principles struggling in the nation at the time, between which there could be no formal or real adjustment, we may learn from the instances of two men,—friends entertaining a sincere and profound respect for each other, both thoroughly honest, and thoroughly able; one of them almost entirely withdrawn from the sphere of political interest and intrigue. Samuel Johnson and Edmund Burke met and conversed at their club. Each day of social intercourse and private study made the one a more thorough type of the most genuine and determined English Tory, the other of the most sagacious and far-seeing Whig. Johnson, of course, had no temptation ever to attempt an alliance with his opponents. Burke had the temptation, yielded to it, and produced the Coalition Ministry, which most men esteemed the great mistake of his life. He believed that he was not sacrificing principle in that act; was maintaining the principle, that the king should be hindered from acting independently of parliament, or of his constitutional advisers. But clearly he illustrated at once the impracticability of any experiments to make Tory and Whig elements sincerely coincide, the great practical influence of the monarch when he has the country to support him, and the danger of his using that influence to gratify a personal prejudice and dislike.

There is much in this century of wearisome Court plots and family intrigues, concerning which it is a privilege to know nothing; so we are often unable to convince ourselves that there was any principle at stake on either side; that the names of place-holders and place-hunters do not supply the only definitions of parties which we need. It is necessary to fight against this plausible opinion, to resist it resolutely, or we shall begin merely to rail at a past age for tempers and habits which may not be worse than our own. I have referred to Johnson and Burke, as proofs that our disparaging phrases, however apparently justified, do not express the whole truth; that there were convictions, real and deep convictions, beneath the hollow surface. But were these convictions adequate for the times in which their strength was greatest? If they could not be brought into fellowship, might there not be some third principle which would demand expression through them or beside them?

When the younger Pitt came into the House of Commons, he seems to have felt strongly, if not distinctly, that it behoved him to assume a position which no Tory or Whig had as yet assumed. His father, he said in his first speech on the Reform of the representation of the House of Commons, had believed it to be the great necessity of the time. This opinion must have been expressed privately in his declining years: it had never been announced to either branch of the legislature. But events which could not be disregarded had been affecting all the calculations of statesmen. The colonies which Lord Chatham hoped in his last hour would be retained as the great ornaments of the British Crown, had been recognised as independent. A new empire in the East had risen to compensate the loss in the West. Maxims as to the nature and origin of Government were suggested by the new world of America; quite other maxims were applied to the old world of Asia. Young men in France and England were busy with discussions about the question which the declaration of independence had raised. If they concerned

England, they must concern the democratical side of its constitution; that must require enlargement and rectification. But the influences from the East especially tended to increase the corruption of the Lower House—to make it—these were Mr. Pitt's own words—nearly as much the representative of the Nabob of Arcot as of the English people. Theories on the origin of Government affected the youthful minister very little; he distinctly disclaimed all sympathy with them. The positive evidence of dishonourable effects, arising from particular interests, like that of the Leadenhall Street Company, and the probability that they would increase, weighed much on his mind; the changes which time and circumstances had produced in the condition of different boroughs, was his second plea for alteration. It is a significant fact that he did not consider a reform in the House needful, as a means of diminishing the influence of the Crown. He entirely approved of the resolution of Mr. Dunning respecting that influence, which the House had adopted during the administration of Lord North. But he said the evil was caused by want of principle in the servants of the Crown; when they were honest, as he believed the successors of Lord North to be, it might be fully redressed. The characteristic feeling of the eighteenth century was thus clearly manifesting itself in the statesman, who was, in some sort, preparing the way for a new state of things, who was giving the first hint of it in his resolution for inquiry into the state of the representation. The need of righteous and wise administration was still accepted by him as the great need of the country. The belief was strong in his mind that it might effect what no legislation and what no changes in the structure of the legislative body could effect.

There were two objections to Mr. Pitt's scheme, one of which may have affected honest statesmen of his own day who had no personal reasons for disliking reform; the other may be more obvious to us. If mere ministerial virtue could control the abuses of the Crown's influence, might not some way be found of curbing those other influences which Mr. Pitt had shown to be so dangerous and more successful, besides that of altering the constitution of the House? It was soon found that some such measure must be devised for bringing the most formidable of these interests under *some* dominion; of what kind it should be the faculties of his two greatest rivals and his own were tasked to discover. Once involved in the question—how England ought to administer the world which the Mogul once ruled—such a field was opened to the politician and the moralist, that inquiries about the places which should or should not return members to the House looked very insignificant. And as Mr. Burke pointed out in his speech on Mr. Fox's India bill, and again and again in the course of the prosecution of Hastings, the right treatment of India, and the punishment of those who turned it merely to their own aggrandisement, would have the most practical reflex operation upon this country; nothing would so much tend to stop the mischief, of which Mr. Pitt had spoken, at its source. Mr. Burke may have believed that his scheme for economical reform on the one hand, and his efforts for justice to our Eastern allies and tributaries on the other, would reform Parliament more than the best attempts to disfranchise one place or enfranchise another. No doubt, also, he was the more indifferent about such measures, because his mind was penetrated with the principle which he announced in his speech at Bristol, that the member for the smallest borough or the largest county is really not member for that borough or county, but for England.

These considerations may have been specially likely to weigh with the men of that time. The one which I said must weigh more powerfully with us is this: Mr. Pitt dwelt much upon the changes which had taken place in the circumstances of the country since writs for knights of the shire and burgesses of the towns were issued. He remarked that the Crown had sometimes interfered to withhold writs, in order to remedy the anomalies which these alterations had occasioned. Was not the exercise of such a discretion very dangerous? Should not the House attempt to provide some measure of its own which should be final as to its principle, though providing for variations in details? Such a measure he thought he could suggest. The counties were least open to corruption. The greatest changes of population had been in the boroughs. What so desirable as to deprive some of them of their representatives, and to bestow the privilege which they had lost upon the shires. Surely a plausible scheme! And now consider how far it would have provided for certain changes which, as we know, were taking place in the country at the very time when Mr. Pitt was ruling it.

2. This was the second subject on which I proposed to speak. We talk of the religious revolution in the sixteenth century, of the political revolution in the seventeenth century. What shall we call that revolution in the eighteenth century which was effected by such men as Arkwright and Watt? Describe their work as mechanical if you will—though the mechanism, in the case of the steam-engine at least, rested upon the acknowledgment of a most mysterious power which had been always working in the universe. Say if you will that the highest thought of those who devised the new machines was that they should increase the profits of those who used them or the material resources of the land. It is not possible, I imagine, for any discoverer, while he is working out his thought, to look so far ahead even as such results; he is too much absorbed in the problem which has been set before him, or in the pure delight of solving it. But let his thoughts have been low or sublime—let them have turned as much or as little as they may upon the kind of blessings or curses of which he might be the author to his fellows—it was

not in his power to hinder that the conception which had gone out of his brain should cause villages to grow into towns; the population of towns to become doubled, trebled, quintupled; places almost solitary to be turned into the hives of a multitude of creatures which were not bees, but which could extract honey, which might also carry stings, which must be under an order and government such as no Parliament could establish.

A new world was coming into existence at this time in the very midst of the old England. The descendants of those who had appeared at different times of our history, claiming some recognition, and who had been dismissed into obscurity, as atoms of which the regular citizen could take no account except when they whirled in strange eddies about him and disturbed his slumbers—these were now demanded by the citizen for his own purposes. He must himself marshal them, and put them in order. They acquire solidity and cohesion under his own hands.

The study of this phenomenon naturally began to occupy thoughtful men. Questions that had been supposed to be settled long ago respecting the condition of trade were reconsidered; the practical conclusions at which men had arrived were disputed and contradicted. Exclusive privileges and monopolies were declared to be mischievous attempts upon the part of human legislators to repeal laws older and more fundamental than their own. Again, as in former days, it is debated whether land is or is not the foundation of a country's wealth. And again the old notion that labour has nearly as much concern in it as the ground itself, started up as the rival hypothesis.

These controversies mainly concerned that which *belonged* to a people; the instrument which it wielded. But what about the men themselves? Could they remain as they had been amidst these great changes? Were they to be left to the operation of material and mechanic forces to grind them or elevate them? Were no moral forces to act upon them? Were they to be destitute of the convictions which had affected so mightily the citizen in former centuries?

It was hard to say whence such a moral force was to come; how such convictions were to be aroused. In the country districts dwelt a body of respectable clergymen, of which a favourable specimen is the chaplain whom Sir Roger de Coverley chose on account of his pleasant voice and his skill in selecting the sermons of the best English divines for his Sunday readings. In the universities and in the higher departments of the Church, were some men of much learning, and some of profound thought, both equally unappreciated by any except men of their own class. The inhabitants of the towns were still much under the influence of the Nonconformist divines, men from whom most of the ruggedness and most of the power of their Puritan ancestors had departed; men reasonably educated, well fitted to keep up the usefulness and respectability of the class which formed their congregations, quite incapable of stirring the heart of any other. The Conformists and Nonconformists both composed an establishment—the first more richly endowed and more acceptable to the upper rank of society, the second more dear to the middle ranks. Which had any message for a set of men who were neither gentry nor tradesmen—but were men nevertheless?

The Wesleys and Whitfield had probably never meditated on the existence of one class or another. They went among colliers in Cornwall, who had a certain organization; among Kingswood thieves, who were chiefly organized for evil purposes. They spoke not to them in that character, but as separate souls, which a Divine Spirit could raise to a new life. But they had themselves been bred in an organized society. They had been called Methodists, for their strict adherence to its rules. The defiance of method which seemed to make that name singularly inappropriate, was itself a step to order. All who were brought under the Wesleyan influence were organized. The Wesleyan rule became a very strict one indeed, tending at one time to absolutism, then to aristocracy, but always with a principle of self-government at the heart of it.

These are important signs of that movement, though far enough from the most important. The acknowledgment of a spiritual power which had practically gone out amongst the most able and thoughtful both of Churchmen and Dissenters, was that which made the Methodist preacher effectual with rich as well as poor—but specially as an instrument of awakening manhood in those who had regarded themselves, and whom others regarded, as mere parts of a mass. The artificial mould into which those whose hearts they had stirred were cast, was a proof that men must find a home in some society, if they have any strong belief stirring in them. The Sect organization could never satisfy the cravings of the age, not even of those who had sought for it. But it contributed to foster a number of influences, which were strong in the age, and which had a political quite as much as a religious significance.

3. Whilst these changes were at work in the outward condition of England, and whilst this influence was acting on its inner life, I do not see what hope there was of a statesman, let his insight or his foresight be as great as it might, arriving at any satisfactory scheme for the reform of the representation. That Mr. Pitt should undertake such a task at his entrance into life, is a pleasing proof that he was not always, as some have said that he was, a full-grown man, that he had many of the audacities and infirmities of youth. He did a great service, as I think, in bringing the subject under the notice of his countrymen. For the time was coming when it would force itself upon them, and we may be glad that they were prepared for it by a statesman so much pledged to the past, so little committed to any

new opinions. But in that age it could only receive a hasty and superficial treatment; no party in the state had any earnest convictions about it. I cannot therefore find fault with Mr. Pitt for relinquishing the task in despair, for not using his ministerial influence to thrust it through the House, for not invoking any strong feeling outside, supposing such a feeling existed, to coerce the majority which opposed him. He was walking more in the steps of his father and of his best predecessors in this century, when he occupied himself with representing the King to the people, than when he strove to devise a scheme by which the people should more effectually represent themselves to the King.

As facts opened upon him, he became more and more aware that the opinions respecting the right of every man to a share of the government, which he had dismissed in his first speech as characteristic of a few fanatics, were those which were mainly enlisted on the side of parliamentary reform. And these opinions were not as he had known them a few years before. They were no longer English, but cosmopolitan; they were connected with the doctrine of the sovereignty of the people, which had been enunciated amidst the hills and lakes of Switzerland, which had been translated into a formula by the constituent assembly, into acts by the mob of Paris. What these things meant Mr. Pitt might not be able to tell. They seemed to mean something very different from the disputes between Whig and Tory politicians which had occupied English statesmen in the eighteenth century; they certainly did not mean what he meant, when he broke to a certain extent through the Whig and Tory traditions, and proposed a scheme which would have made the landed interest in the House more powerful. Maxims essentially different from his own were associated with his measures. He abandoned the measures rather than be committed to the maxims; if his repudiation ultimately took a very vehement shape, those who had fancied him their champion and fellow-worker might fairly complain, but after times will not accuse him of any serious inconsistency.

Mr. Fox, who had honourably supported the reforming propositions of his rival, had not the same motive for changing his course. He had strong French sympathies; the phrase Sovereignty of the People did not startle him; he was inclined to adopt it, as if it signified little more than the deposition of James II. had signified. Though outrageous acts might accompany the demand for liberty by the clubs of Paris, the word had for him essentially a Whig sound; his Whig instincts led him to accept it from whatever nation it proceeded.

Mr. Burke perceived keenly the confusion which lay in this word—the utter difference, nay, the absolute contrast between the ideas of the English and the French Revolution. His Whiggism, he said, bound him to a reverence for old charters, and to a recognition of history. Every appeal of those who complained of arbitrary government, in the age of arbitrary government, had been to an existing constitution which had been violated. In France, charters were set at naught, history was disclaimed, the world was to begin again at the end of the eighteenth century. The evidence which he produced for these propositions was, it seems to me, irresistible; those who tried to patch the old garment of Whiggism with the new cloth of the Declaration of the Right must produce a hopeless rent. And was he not doing a useful work in trying to keep that old garment entire? Could it be dispensed with or cast aside as useless? I believe that his vindication of the worth of the old was necessary before England could profit by any of those lessons which God intended us to learn from the new world which was coming to birth amidst such throes and agonies. If the people was to be more a people than it had been, it must learn its foundations were laid centuries ago; a republic which announced itself in the year One, must die before it was out of its cradle.

Such a testimony, I conceive, was not only, not chiefly, good for those who had lands and gold, and who feared that these might be taken from them. They might eagerly quote Burke's phrase about "the swinish multitude." They might think that all fell under that description who had not lands or gold, that none came within it who had. If they had understood Burke better, they would have seen that he was pleading for ancient laws which had been the protection of poor and rich, which had asserted for both a position in the commonwealth. If they had known history as well as he did, they would have been aware that men with lands and gold had continually tampered with laws for their own ends; that they had found laws great impediments to their self-indulgence; that they had often exhibited a very "swinish" inclination to trample them under foot. Alas! Burke did not help them to read—could not read himself—these lessons written afresh in letters of blood on the records of the French Revolution. He could talk foolishly and irreverently of "vice losing half its evil in losing all its grossness," not recollecting how gross, how "swinish" had been many of the vices of the French nobility and the French Court. He could bestow a generous and just pity upon the sorrows of the noble Queen of France; a pity, generous, at least, and partly just, on the sorrows of the emigrants, priests, and lords. He did not own that if they had done something to raise the multitude above the condition of a mob into the condition of a people, they might never have been obliged to fly from a land which would have confessed the worth and blessedness of their influence. Burke could complain, as the pulpits of England complained, of French atheism. He and they forgot how much there was of atheism in refusing to confess the Divine hand in these judgments; how much they were glorifying the sovereignty which they denied, if they supposed that it could overthrow a society that was good and healthy—that had not become corrupt and rotten.

These were not lessons to be learnt at once,—or to be learnt at all for the sake of diminishing the charity of England towards the sufferers of any class or nation. They were lessons which she had to lay to her own heart, to turn to her own use. If she tried to do that, she might profit equally by the stern admonitions of Burke, which appeared to crush all hope from the French Revolution, and by the warmest and most passionate of these hopes. It may be strange to pass from his " Reflections " to such lines as these, and yet I own to a profound sympathy with both, and to a firm belief that both had a foundation in truth :

> " Oh, pleasant exercise of hope and joy!
> For mighty were the auxiliars which then stood
> Upon our side, we who were strong in love!
> Bliss was it in that dawn to be alive,
> But to be young was very heaven! O times!
> In which the meagre, stale, forbidding ways
> Of custom, law, and statute, took at once
> The attraction of a country in romance!
> When Reason seemed the most to assert her rights,
> When most intent on making of herself
> A prime Enchantress—to assist the work
> Which then was going forward in her name!
> Not favoured spots alone, but the whole earth,
> The beauty wore of promise—that which sets
> (As at some moments might not be unfelt
> Amidst the bowers of Paradise itself)
> The budding rose above the rose full blown.
> What temper at the prospect did not wake
> To happiness unthought of? The inert
> Were roused, and lively natures rapt away!
> They who had fed their childhood upon dreams,

> The playfellows of Fancy—who had made
> All powers of swiftness, subtlety, and strength,
> Their ministers—who in lordly wise had stirred
> Among the grandest objects of the sense,
> And dealt with whatsoever they found there
> As if they had within some lurking right
> To wield it;—they, too, who of gentler mood
> Had watched all gentle motions, and to these
> Had fitted their own thoughts, schemers more mild,
> And in the region of their peaceful selves;—
> Now was it that both found, the meek and lofty
> Did both find helpers to their hearts' desire,
> And stuff at hand, plastic as they could wish,—
> Were called upon to exercise their skill,
> Not in Utopia—subterraneous fields—
> Or some secreted island, Heaven knows where!
> But in the very world, which is the world
> Of all of us—the place where in the end
> We find our happiness, or not at all!"

If these were the visions of youth, they were visions which an old, grave, conservative poet registered as some of the most precious of his life, as linked to all its hardest battles, to its truest humanity. Can they have been disappointed? Must not the bitter disappointments which those who cherished them were called to undergo have been for the very purpose of showing them the substance which lay behind all that looked, all that was, fantastical in these expectations?

One hint I will offer before I finish this chapter, which may lead us to pause before we assume that Wordsworth and such as he must have been deluded in supposing that an age was beginning in which man, as man, should have an honour which custom, law, and statute had not hitherto recognised. Among many indications which I should dwell upon of the difference between the standard of political morality in the latter part of the eighteenth century and in the beginning of it, there is one which few will now be inclined to dispute. The zeal of Burke and Fox to inquire into Indian delinquencies may, though I think quite unjustly, be interpreted into a desire for a grand opportunity of rhetorical display. The motion of Mr. Wilberforce for the abolition of the slave trade will be accepted as a sign that a question not concerning party—a question of human interests —could engage the sympathies of the greatest men of all parties. That Mr. Wilberforce himself was moved to undertake this cause by his sense of the sacredness of every human being, of whatever colour —that he had derived this sense from those teachers who were called Methodists by the common public— will not be denied. But it is equally certain that, though he was the personal friend of Mr. Pitt, though he went cordially with him in all his denunciations of Jacobinism, Mr. Wilberforce was charged by every advocate of the West India interest with sanctioning the doctrine of the Rights of Man. How could he or his disciples vindicate themselves from the accusation? Were they not taking one of the lowest specimens of the race, and asserting—in their popular appeals—in the pictures that were meant to move the common English feeling—that he was a brother as well as a man? Was not this fraternity? Was not this equality? Mr. Wilberforce might feel

—might be sure—that the difference, the opposition common between him and those who used these phrases in France, was as great as it could be. But how was he to make the difference, the opposition, manifest? On what ground did he assert the humanity, the brotherhood of the slave? Was it a ground which interfered with the honour of the freeman? This was a question which the next age would have earnestly to consider, which might affect profoundly all its thoughts respecting the education and representation of the English people.

CHAPTER VI.

THE HOUSE OF COMMONS IN THE NINETEENTH CENTURY.

I READ to you at the close of the last chapter some verses describing, as I believe, most faithfully the emotions with which a number of young Englishmen welcomed the outburst of the French Revolution. It is often said that those emotions were transitory; that in a number of persons, in the writer of these lines conspicuously, they were followed by a violent reaction towards an exclusively national temper, even towards a vehement Toryism. That, we are told, was the fruit of all this passionate delight, these fervid expectations; a humiliating sense of delusion, a return to an old superstition. The moral, of course, is, "Beware of any strong belief, of any great enthusiasm. Keep the level road. Steer safely between extremes." I am aware how strong is the apparent evidence for these assertions, how much attraction there is in a critical and contemptuous age towards the inference. But I fancy that the critics are open to the charge which they would repudiate the most. They have not sifted the evidence. Their wishes, not their reasons, have suggested the conclusion. If the history of these alleged reactions is fairly examined, it will be found, as the writer of the verses whom I quoted has sung, that there are—

> "Thoughts which wake
> To perish never,
> Which neither listlessness nor mad endeavour,
> Nor man nor boy,
> Nor aught which is at enmity with joy,
> Can utterly abolish or destroy."

It will be found that there has been a great result from the enthusiasm which is supposed to have been abortive. I do not say that the opposite temper has no reward. I am sure that it has. It adds greatly to the self-complacency of its possessor; it procures him considerable credit for sagacity with his contemporaries. If it produces no great good to mankind, he may fairly boast that he never aimed at producing any. And he is useful "beyond the intention of his thought" in this way; he detects and cultivates the enthusiasm which no scorn can quench, which thrives best in the roughest weather.

The first thought in men trained like Wordsworth, when they heard of the downfall of the Bastile, was this: "A nation which has been struggling with unspeakable oppressions, has declared itself *free*. The name which is dearest to Englishmen, has been claimed by those whom we counted our natural enemies, by a nation grown old in luxury. Such emancipations are rare. Yet there have been examples of the recovery of a lost inheritance. But here is a country not content with the blessing for itself; it would share the blessing with all nations. There is no rivalry, no jealousy. It longs to give what it had received. Is not this a new impulse? Is it not a sign that the age, not of national freedom only, but of human freedom, is setting in?"

Then there was another side to this great movement. The apostle of it had published a new Code. Education, he said, had been used to counteract Nature. The most artificial, the more cruel system, had been accounted the wisest. Ought not Nature to be the guide of all our discipline? Should not our desire be to give it play—not to contract and coerce it? Evidently this was a further step in the emancipation. It went to the root of society. It entered into the household. It connected the free life of the man with the free life of the child.

Thirdly, The old maxim of Louis XIV., which had been felt in England to be at variance with all our constitutional doctrines, " I am the state," had now encountered its formal direct contradiction. Rousseau had taught the French to say, " We are the state. We are the sovereign. There may be nobles, kings, even priests, if we please. But we appoint them. They hold their commissions from us."

These we may take as the three dogmas of the Revolution. They could not remain dogmas. They burst forth at once into life and practice. They appealed, as Mr. Wordsworth showed us, to the intellect and imagination at once. They linked reason to romance. They gave the promise of an age which should supplant the age of dry law, and custom, and tradition.

I. The first was the one which came into the most immediate manifestation. The conspiracy of the allies against France called it out. The monarchs would put down the Republic. The Republic would deliver the nations from the monarchs. What field for the experiment so brilliant and glorious as Italy? What defiance so great as one which should comprehend its princes, its aristocracies, the Austrian, the Pope? The defiance is hurled forth. It is made good. The young soldier of the Republic wins for France, and for himself, such laurels as none had won for centuries. Then he aspires to join the Mohammedan with the Christian, to bestow on Egypt the same freedom as on Europe.

And then this hero of Italy, this reconciler of creeds, becomes the first consul, becomes the emperor. A monarch, then, after all, is to establish the brotherhood of the nations. Their freedom means that they bow down to him. That he understands to be his destiny. He must fulfil the idea of the Revolution. He must destroy the barriers which divide the nations. He must make them portions of one grand democracy which has, as the Roman democracy had, a general at its head. It is, he says, his destiny; he appears to prove that it is. Kingdoms and empires actually stoop to him. The nation which Frederick the Great had raised crumbles under his feet. The German empire ceases, for it cannot stand beside his empire. At Tilsit Napoleon and Alexander consider how they may divide the world between them.

And this, then, said those who had hailed the first awaking of a nation to freedom—who had hailed with still more rapture its promises of freedom to all nations — this, then, was the idea of the French Revolution! Thus, even thus, it is realised. If you will turn from Wordsworth's description of his feelings at the commencement of the Revolution to his "Sonnets to Liberty," you will see this process of reaction in its different stages. I scarcely know a more interesting or affecting study, or one which more connects the biography of a recluse—as he had a right to call himself—with English and European history. The sentiment of liberty was the very one which the Revolution had kindled. Whatever other applications there might be of the word, that which connected it with the Nation was the most simple, the most obvious. To an Englishman the connection was inevitable. England had lived—when its life had been most vigorous—to resist all experiments of universal government which had interfered with its distinctiveness as a people. The pope, Philip II., Louis XIV., all had alike been fought with on this ground. No general language, it had been said, shall rob us of our language, no imperial or spiritual head shall hinder us from recognising our own king as supreme in the fullest sense of the word. All faith in a living God had, as I have shown you before, been bound up with faith in this national freedom. It was, no doubt, a sore trial, a shock to the inmost soul, to part with the dream that France was to regenerate the universe. But was it not fidelity to one's deepest convictions to resist her in the name of national freedom? No doubt after a time of painful numbness there was the pleasant sense that the old English belief was returning; that traditions were not worthless if they were traditions of deeds done, of victories achieved on behalf of the very cause which had first enlisted our sympathies for the foreign people. But there was no need to abandon the larger hopes which the Revolution had created. Was not England taking the very part which France had claimed for herself? In opposing Napoleon was not she preaching liberty to the nations? Could she help Spain and Portugal with any watchword but that? Nay, was it not beginning to be heard through every part of Europe? Did not Prussia call forth her sons in that name? Did not Austria herself—with whatever feebleness and uncertainty—at last pronounce it? Was it not heard from the Kremlin of Moscow? Did not the Autocrat of all the Russias relinquish his vision of sharing the world with Napoleon, and invoke the nations in God's name to cast off a yoke which they could not bear?

That the monarchs, whose object, in 1792, had been to stifle the cry for liberty, which they thought would spread from France into their countries, should one after another join themselves in the cry, till the words "battle of the nations" should be chosen to describe their struggle, must surely have seemed a triumph to those who had protested most strongly against the convention of Pilnitz and the manifesto of the Duke of Brunswick. If the parties had shifted their colours—if the advocates for Imperialism had become the leaders of the war against Imperialism—if those who had begun with proclaiming the rights of nations and of men had been the instruments of trampling them down—this change could not affect the consistency of men who, through good and evil report, had maintained Imperialism to be a curse, who had rejoiced whenever nations had discovered their own strength and shaken it off.

There were, however, various dangers awaiting this consistency. First, there was the danger of overlooking the multitude of old and scandalous abuses in the different countries, as well as the immorality of their different rulers which had caused the victory of the imperial arms, and on which they had executed a predestined vengeance. It was well, no doubt, to forgive and forget past offences, to give the rulers credit for a desire to begin a new career. But it was not well to reject the divine warnings of twenty years. It was not well to deny the blessings which the hurricane of these twenty years had produced, by sweeping away that which must have hindered all fresh growth. There was another danger resulting from the feebleness and wrong-doings of these nations which had revolted against the oppressor. Wordsworth had said that the power of armies was a visible thing, but that none could measure the invisible strength which there was in a people rising as the Spaniards rose. Our soldiers came back and told us that this supposed invisible strength had been connected with contempt of discipline, with great savageness and great treachery. The organic force of armies had proved itself much mightier and much nobler. So spoke men who could not be suspected of contempt for any popular cause, any lurking passion for monarchies or aristocracies; such men as Colonel William Napier. These reports must have produced a distrust in all so-called national movements, a belief that they tended to anarchy. Then, thirdly, it had been notorious that the Whig party in England had been far less interested in the war against Napoleon than their opponents, that some of them had even expressed a sympathy with him. Hence those who held the sentiments that are embodied in Wordsworth's Sonnets, were drawn forcibly into alliance with the party which had a nervous dread of the word " liberty." That one who had writen as he wrote about Milton and the times of the Commonwealth, about Toussaint and the patriots of St. Domingo, should become identified with the school of repression, struck many as a flagrant revolt from his original principle. They did not see how much it was the effect of his circumstances. Dislike for a party to which he had never belonged—which was identified in his mind with indifference to a cause that had been to him a passion—the most prominent and admired writers in which had been contemptuous opposers of his poetical reforms—drove him almost inevitably into sympathy with their opponents; for men as they grow older want some friends and allies to compensate the loss of youthful vigour, and may overlook much to procure them. Mr. Wordsworth had other compensations. He saw those maxims respecting the dignity of the peasant and of his speech, respecting the meanness of the artificial diction which had been called poetical—maxims savouring of his French as well as of his English faith—sullenly accepted in the very classes to which they were most offensive, determining consciously the feelings and thoughts of young men in England and America, moulding the poetry of a new generation. He needed such comfort; for the time which followed the peace, the time of the Holy Alliance and of our Regency, was not one in which it was easy to feel that to be alive was joy, that to be young was very heaven. It was a time of terrible exhaustion. The past seemed past indeed; the future had a very leaden aspect. Efforts at repression were the great and successful efforts. That the nations should not open their eyes, or peep, or breathe, appeared to be the desire of those monarchs who had encouraged them to such preternatural activity against the French Emperor. And yet the Holy Alliance was itself a testimony that the French had dreamed a dream which would be fulfilled. " There must be a union of nations—a common law of nations—a great fraternity," said the enthusiasts. " There shall be such a union, such a fraternity," said the monarchs. " *We* will create it, and put ourselves at the head of it." Not a successful experiment more than that of the republic, more than that of the empire; one very perplexing, very unintelligible to those who had entertained the idea of fraternity; to those who had thought it must be associated with liberty for each nation. But certainly a sign of what the age was aiming at; certainly a witness that the thought which had been awakened in it was one that could not perish; that there must be recognised somehow a general humanity as well as a distinct national life. *Somehow*, though not, it would seem, by any of these methods; the monarchs had proved that. " We must have the nations alive," they said at one moment. " We must kill them to get a general alliance," they said afterwards. They alternately accepted and denied each side of the gorgeous vision, showing they had not discovered how either side should be realized.

Theirs was, they said, a *Holy* Alliance. The epithet sounded hypocritical to the people who heard it; most of the acts which accompanied it justified the imputation. It was adopted in opposition to the atheism of the revolution; often it seemed to be a perpetuation of that atheism. Did the monarchs confess a

Divine Ruler, or did they think they *were* the divine rulers; that the power of God was vested in them—was absorbed into them; that they could reconstruct and remould his universe? They hovered between these two opinions; there were times when they yielded to all the blasphemy of the second idea; there were times when they rose to the truth of the first. They left a witness that the second could not be true; for what came of their reconstruction and remoulding; what proof did they give of their creative power? They left a witness in the name which they assumed, that there is a Sovereign holy and just, not merely powerful, who might care more for the nations than they did, who might design to bind them into one.

The man who had most of this idea in its truth and in its perversion—the real former and soul of the Alliance, Alexander of Russia, left the world. Then its impotence began to appear. To Metternich and his Austrians it was merely a diplomatic invention. As such Mr. Canning, when foreign minister of England, shook it off. The stirrings of the nations which had never ceased, but which had been crushed as anarchical, and which had proved themselves to be feeble, became more hopeful. France, which had restored absolutism in Spain, became again impatient of the tendency to it in herself. There was concession, there was more violent repression. Charles X. tried his *coup d'état*, and the second French Revolution revived for a moment some of the fears and hopes which had been called forth by the first.

STATE OF FRANCE AND ENGLAND. 179

The fears were soon quelled. Louis Philippe took his place among the recognised monarchs of Europe. He was found to have no grand imagination of disturbing or regenerating the nations. His ambition was to discover the best means of keeping in order the discontent that was stirring in his own. The hopes were not so manageable. A government directed by a skilful head, with many able subordinates—a government possessing the confidence of the mercantile classes, and securing a material prosperity—did not satisfy all the cravings of a nation which had aspired to lead the world into freedom and order. The thought of a distinct national life, the thought of a common brotherhood for the nations— these were not dead during the reign of Louis Philippe. They were felt in France amidst all its materialism, they could not be extinguished in England by all our railway speculations. There they gave birth to republican conspiracies and to ecclesiastical schemes, which appeared to be most alien from republicanism. Passionate efforts there were in this time to recover the freedom for France which the Revolution had claimed, which the citizen king was said to be stifling; passionate efforts to recover an idea older than the Revolution, the idea of a spiritual government or universal society. Chartist movements in England were a feeble reproduction of the first; they testified that the middle class ascendancy was not satisfactory to all classes in the community. The cries for a spiritual fellowship, which were heard more distinctly, expressed a similar discontent on other grounds. " The Parliament," it was said, " is wholly secular, wholly commmercial. Yet it holds the Church and all divine interests under its yoke. Here or elsewhere, in the past if not in the present, we must find some higher authority, one to which we can bow without feeling that we are mere children of this world." In some these cries exhausted themselves in mere protests against the vulgar practicality of the English mind, in a search for the picturesque. In some they became thoroughly practical as to their nature and in their results. In both countries, modern and ancient opinions and aspirations were often curiously blended. A Church was demanded which should be emphatically for the poor—in which all should be on a level. The new Jacobinism of the Revolution combined itself with the old Jacobinism of the Dominican. Men who had abhorred democracy felt the power of it, and allowed it through one entrance or another to come into their minds, almost to possess them.

The sudden downfall of that kingdom which had appeared to stand so firmly on its material basis, gave another turn to these speculations and a greater impulse to them than before. The formation of a new republic, the appearance of a new empire, have compelled us once more to collect all the experiences, to marshall all the convictions, which have taught us how an empire tries to satisfy the demands for a universal society; how inevitably it slays the nation to satisfy them. The struggles of the empire with the popedom oblige us to ask ourselves whether there must not be something hidden behind that notion of a paternal rule which the Holy Alliance tried to embody, that might harmonise with the freedom of distinct peoples; whether that hidden something may not be the old confession of a God who makes free, and therefore who cannot sanction the efforts of emperors or popes to make slaves? So far, then, as this first idea or dogma of the revolution is concerned —that which affirms the existençe of a humanity as well as of a distinct national life—I think we have proof enough that it is one which

> "Neither listlessness nor mad endeavour,
> Nor aught which is at enmity with joy,
> Can utterly abolish or destroy."

II. The second dogma of the French Revolution related, I said, to Education. It connected the education of the child with the life of the citizen. The nineteenth century has certainly never lost sight of this connexion. Each party has acknowledged it; each has attempted to show that it can establish and realise the connexion as no other can. This problem has been the great trial of the age. We all feel that no political problem can be solved completely, unless it be solved. But the question of education assumed a special form in the minds of those who had most influence on the revolutionary movement. It was the same form which we find in all the phrases of the time: "Man is naturally free—man has natural rights;" that was the premiss. "Artificial society has robbed him of his freedom—has cheated him of his rights. Bring him back to Nature, that he may recover them;" that was the practical conclusion.

Now, there were in England no persons who felt and recognised the importance of education more than the authors of the religious movement to which I referred in my last chapter. There were none who more desired that education should be extended to all classes. But there were also none who demurred more to the phraseology which took it for granted that education ought to follow Nature—that the nature of the man, or of the child, could in the least be trusted or treated as good. It was, they said, not good, but evil; not to be obeyed, but to be subdued or changed. This was that contrast to which I alluded in the last chapter, as leading to so many curious perplexities with reference to the question of the slave. He has been robbed of his natural liberty, said the champion of the French Declaration. He is a man and a brother, said the supporter of Mr. Wilberforce. Well! are not the expressions equivalent? May not they be interchanged? Continually they *were* interchanged in rhetorical speeches, even in elaborate arguments. Their opponents confounded them. Those who used them often could not distinguish them. Only when it came to this test of education, and the way in which they were to be applied, either to the African or the Englishman, the difference became manifest; it was found that there was a wide gulf between opinions which seemed to be identical.

There was another idea distinct from both of these which had been long at work in England. It was the idea of our public-school education. Why was the boy sent to school? To be under masters who would fit him for the exercise of his functions as a freeman, as a citizen. He must be subjected to laws; he must be punished if he disobeys the laws. He is in a society; in the order of that society he will learn some of the conditions to which he must submit when he comes into the larger society of the nation; —what his relations will be to the other members of it—what laws will bind him when he hears no more a voice bidding him do this, or not do that—what sentences may await him when there is no longer a rod visibly hanging before him. Here is a scheme of education very unlike that which prescribes the following of Nature. Its abuses supplied some of the strongest arguments to those who urged that as the great principle of reformation. But, on the other hand, it was anything but satisfactory to those who based all their thoughts of man on the corruption of human nature. This school system, it seemed to them, gave scope and play to many of the worst passions of our nature. " Must not these," it was asked, "always receive encouragement and development in a society not carefully weeded and sifted, or else continually watched ? Is it not the duty of a parent who does not wish to train his child for the acquisition of worldly feelings and habits, to keep him under his own eye? Evils, no doubt, must be encountered, but they will not be aggravated in each boy by continual contact with the evils in his fellows."

Whatever maxims of the kind any parent of the upper or middle class might adopt in reference to his own children, it is clear that they were not applicable to the poorer classes. And now was the time when the condition of these classes must be faced, when all that amazing development of manufacturing industry and power which I said would derange political calculations, must be contemplated in reference to this question also. Evidently the provisions for instruction which had been made in former days, numerous as they were, elaborately as some of them had been contrived to meet the circumstances of their own time, did not in the least anticipate this alteration. Evidently, too, the agricultural labourers, from whatever change in manners, from whatever neglect of those who should have cared for them, were at least as much in need of teaching as the mechanics. How must the case of either be treated?

It was almost inevitable that when such large bodies had to be considered, some of the first contrivances should concern the way in which they could be packed together in a room, and in which maxims of organisation might be applied to them. It was an important preliminary question; it never could become an indifferent one. Most especially it could not be indifferent if the old English doctrine were in any degree the true one. The order of a school must then not be merely a condition of its efficiency; it must be a substantive part of the lesson conveyed in the school—perhaps not the least important part. Whatever else might be done for boys or girls, some sort of drill, or military discipline and exercise, must at all events be secured for them. But what was to be taught these children? who were to teach them? The first inquiry has given rise to all those controversies about religious and secular teaching, and about different kinds of religious and secular teachings, by which our time has been distracted; the second, to the controversies whether the State or the Established Church, or different denominations, should be intrusted with the work. I need not say how many arguments have been produced in favour of each of these courses—how satisfied each reasoner is that he has confuted his adversary and established his own conclusion. But since something has had to be done, and it has been impossible to wait till one of the theories conquered the other, children have received purely religious instruction in some schools, and what is called purely secular instruction in some others, and what is called mixed religious and secular teaching in a third. They have received lessons from clergymen of the English Church, and lessons from all classes of the Dissenters, each imparting what seemed to them the right kind of religious lesson. And the State has gradually assumed a general superintendence over all three; not forcing them into a particular groove, but stimulating the energies of each, and making what it can of them all together, deeming that thus it was doing what it could to form English citizens.

I do not see how we can find fault with any arrangements which are the best that are to be had, or how we can wish any effort which is at work suspended till some other, which may strike us as more reasonable or efficient, be put into its place. I rather think that in this seeming medley of parties and influences, in their oppositions and attempts at combination, we have a sign of what this age is, and how it differs from the last. Then a union of parties, it seemed, could only result in the loss of the principle which each maintained. In our time there is an evident consciousness in each of any two contending parties that its own conclusions and position are not altogether satisfactory, Something must be borrowed from the other, or a third principle must be discovered which they must agree to denounce, or else in which they must try to coalesce. Unity is always escaping them, but it must be pursued.

I do not anticipate any union for those who are disputing about kinds of teaching, or for the persons who are to teach, or even for the children or men who are to be taught, till those who hold the opposite dogmas about Nature to which I have referred, shall come to some adjustment of their differences, to some truth that will harmonise *them*. I cannot but see

THE VICTORY OVER NATURE.

that Rousseau's denunciations of unnatural education have had an immense effect upon the thought of this age, upon every man and woman who has given any consideration to the subject. All the questions which Pestalozzi raised about the development of the faculties—his practical efforts to bring forth that which is within the child instead of merely forcing something upon it—received their direction from this hint. All the protests against the system of terror which had become so prevalent in our schools may be traced to that influence. Miss Edgeworth's methods of scientific training were no doubt greatly affected by it, if they were not derived from it. Every attempt to connect external teaching with the life and experience of the subject of the teaching bears witness to it. Still more evidently the denunciations of artificial diction by Wordsworth, mixed as they were with a continual tendency towards the worship of Nature, stood in the closest relation to the maxims of Rousseau. But Wordsworth was preserved from the full influence of those maxims partly by his abhorrence of the Della Cruscan school, which adopted them; partly by his severe life; partly by his sympathy with the actual peasant. Where naturalness was pursued as a principle, it became, in the majority of cases, not art, but artifice; where the man enthroned natural impulses as his lords and masters, he became an ignominious, degraded man.

Here, then, we may find the vindication of the protest which the school that followed Wesley has uttered against the natural man. He is not the true man. He is not the free man. He has stooped to inclinations and tendencies which he was intended to rule. He has sunk into the savage or the serf condition. The citizen, the freeman, can never recognise THAT as the human condition. It is the very reverse of the human condition. It is the condition of the man who is trying to be a solitary, selfish creature, who is forgetting that he is one of a kind. The old doctrine of education, which treats humane studies as those which distinguish the cultivated man from the uncultivated, confesses that cultivation is for man, not for any specific class of men. Here is the truth, then, of that lesson which the French Revolution has bequeathed to us, separated from its confused phraseology, separated from a notion which has debased and vulgarised it. Here we get a glimpse of the distinction between ʋne acknowledgment of the slave as one capable of citizenship and manhood, and therefore never to be treated as a chattel, and the doctrine which would make the grovelling state of the slave or of the savage the measure by which we estimate the man. The true education surely is that which assumes that every boy and every man has need to conquer his selfish nature, to rise out of it, to acquire the true humanity. Whatever teaching most assures him that he can do that, whatever most explains to him the help that he has for doing it, must be the best for the citizen and the man. I do not pronounce who could best impart such an education; but I think if we would fulfil the dream of the French Revolution, we must find some way of making our pupils understand that there is a manhood for them all into whatever class they are born. And I think that here, as in the last case, the proclamation of a God who would raise them to the possession of that manhood, must be that which they want more than all lessons secular or religious, ecclesiastical or sectarian, which proceed upon any other basis.

III. I pass to the third of these revolutionary dogmas, the one which lays down the sovereignty of the people as the interpretation of all government and all society. That toast, "the sovereignty of the people," was given once by the Duke of Norfolk, or Lord Stanhope, and accepted by Mr. Fox, at a London dinner. What precise sense these eminent men attached to the phrase, I do not know. If they regarded it merely as a rhetorical phrase, they were surely much mistaken. They were playing with edged tools. The words had been associated with every act and scene of the French drama. They signified that the Third Estate was *the* estate of the realm, that the other (so called) estates were of necessity and by an everlasting law subject to that which was the most numerous. In this sense the statement must have been understood by those who took it seriously in England. It was not an exaggeration of any old sentiment about the right to depose monarchs. It struck at the noble even more than at the monarch. The Whig, who had always regarded the aristocracy as a main barrier against royal oppression, could not adopt that sentiment without deserting those which had been most dear and sacred to him.

This fact soon became very clear to the most distinguished and enlightened members of Mr. Fox's party. Mr. Grey had presented the petition of the friends of the people. No doubt those who signed that petition had various opinions. Some wished for parliamentary reform that they might invest the third estate with its sovereignty. Some only wished, as Mr. Pitt had wished, to remove blots and scandals from the old constitution. This confusion of objects continued in the supporters of reform afterwards. But their illustrious advocate stood aloof from them. Between the years 1793 and 1830, hardly any one would have associated him with this cause. He was the eloquent advocate of the Roman Catholic claims. He was the opponent of the measures for restraining the press and suspending the Habeas Corpus Act. But all propositions for reform in the House of Commons fell into the hands of Sir Francis Burdett, who denounced Lord Grey and the Whigs no less than the Tories. The new class of Radical reformers—party they refused to call themselves—was forming itself very slowly. Its maxims were not clearly defined. Sir Francis Burdett was a vehement admirer of Magna Charta; though the idol of a great city, his sympathies were with the land. But he was nearly alone in the House. He often divided with one other member in his motions for inquiry into the state of the representation, or for any specific change. Those who supported him outside of the House had a general conviction that it was corrupt, and that to set it right would be to set the nation right. They did not, perhaps, know themselves whether they wished to restore an old edifice, or to build a new one. In times of distress, the cry for reform among the suffering class assumed a revolutionary character; it was a cry for bread. Then came schemes for putting down seditious acts and words; supported commonly by the prosperous members of the middle class; increasing the disaffection of the lower.

I do not imagine that the doctrine of the sovereignty of the people penetrated deeply into the minds of Englishmen during the reign of George III.; there was a habitual respect for the actual king which interfered with the spread of it. After the accession of George IV., especially after the trial of the queen, it must have made much more way; an energetic leader might cause it to take shape in the words or acts of a mob. But when it did take that shape, there was the interest of the middle class to fight against it. There came a time, however, when the middle class began to share this feeling. A set of men joined the ranks of the Radical reformers in the House of Commons, who specially represented the temper of this class—men free from all fancy—devoted to figures—careful in noting and checking official abuses—indifferent to the traditions of the past—incredulous of anything but statistics—apt to measure all things by a pecuniary standard, but faithful and honest in the use of that standard. Such men had little in common with the reformers who spoke of Magna Charta and the Bill of Rights. Being more patient of details, and more occupied with the present, they acquired an influence which the others did not possess. They held that a better representation would promote economy and diminish taxation. And presently they learned from men more educated and philosophical than they were, on what principles they might defend it.

For more than half a century, Mr. Bentham had been sending forth books on morals and jurisprudence. They had been translated from his own expressive and characteristic, but singular dialect, into thoroughly readable French by M. Dumont; in that form they had exercised an influence abroad which they had only possessed here over a few minds. They had a French side and an English side. The doctrine of the Revolution, that a man has any natural rights before he enters into society, was utterly discarded; all that romance which had delighted the early enthusiasts was stripped off; so Mr. Bentham did homage to the habits and instincts of the English citizen. But not only romance disappeared in his hands. The old English belief that the life of a people is a continuous life—the dream of a nation as anything but the sum of its inhabitants at any given time—was also scattered to the winds. The greatest happiness of the greatest number—the will of the majority—

THE CHANGE IN OPINION.

these were the formulas under which all ideas of society and government were comprehended; what could not be reduced to these must be fiction. The bare enunciation of such propositions could not in itself have commanded the assent or the reverence of men busy with all the details of life. But Mr. Bentham had an immense skill in grappling with details; he had gone laboriously into the legal practices and customary opinions which contradicted, or seemed to him to contradict, his primary dogmas; he had shown what a number of private and particular interests clashed with the general interests; he had explained how all governments might be made into a scheme of checks upon these interests. Men who had leisure for examining his exposures of abuses, and his suggestions of plans, came away with a high conception of him as a practical reformer. Those who had not this leisure, read his conclusions in manageable treatises by able men thoroughly imbued with his principles, who laid bare with singular cleverness the sophisms and inconsistencies of both the English schools. Treatises of this kind were eagerly devoured by many who had grown to be weary of party government; the Radical Reformers, from being treated as visionaries and fanatics, became suddenly respected and feared as rigid and consistent logicians. Thus France had won a singular triumph. The idea of the sovereignty of the people—that is to say, of the greatest number — had vanquished that class of Englishmen which cared least about ideas. And this class was soon to show what power was in it, how it could convert some who were naturally least in sympathy with it, into its servants.

Unexpected circumstances helped forward the victory. The claims of the Roman Catholics had been supported by Mr. Pitt. His distinguished pupil, Mr. Canning, inherited his opinions on that subject, as on many others. The Whigs had supported the cause consistently and unanimously; so alienating themselves from the Sovereign, and setting themselves at war with a considerable section of the middle class. And now these claims were suddenly conceded by the minister whose whole life had been spent in opposing them. Apparently he yielded to a strong organization—to the manifested conviction of the Irish people. Such an example made, no doubt, a strong impression upon that part of the English people which cared more for reform in the House of Commons, than for any relief to Roman Catholics. But it operated also in another way. It produced in the Tory party a disgust for their leaders—a notion that great changes in the constitution of Parliament had been made already, and that it was no longer that body which they had wished to keep untouched. These Tories were not unwilling to let the Whig leaders drive out those who had lost their confidence; though, whether it should be given to them, must depend on the course which they followed and the allies which they chose.

The choice of allies—even the determination of a

course—is seldom left to the will of statesmen. It might have been predicted by some who looked for a dramatic harmony in a man's life, that the Mr. Grey of 1793 would crown his life, after years of absence from office, by introducing some measure of reform. It could *not* have been predicted that one of the most lofty of aristocratical leaders should introduce a measure, expressing very faithfully the feelings of the middle class, and giving it a position which would enable it to govern to a great extent, the movements of the State, even the action of the other assembly. But the revolution of 1830 in France had, as I said, proclaimed the ascendancy of that class there. A Reform Bill of 1831 could do little more than affirm the same ascendancy here.

Was this bill, then, at variance with the old maxims of the English constitution? Those who studied it in a strictly antiquarian spirit felt that it was. The distinctions of freeholder and freeman, which had been the great distinctions in our representation, were nominally preserved in the distinction of counties and towns. But so little was the idea of the freeholder recognised, that by a strange clause, introduced by a Tory who valued himself on his adherence to old maxims, accepted by Radicals who desired the independence of electors—tenants at will, the direct opposite of freeholders, were admitted to the county franchise. On the other hand, what was there in the mere fact of a man paying ten pounds a year for a house which connected him with the old freeman, the member of some organised guild or company? Looked at in this aspect, the bill would seem to be a very wide departure from the ancient order. Again, the ideas of numerical representation and money representation mingled confusedly in it; one cannot affirm distinctly which is the predominant one. That would appear not to be an antiquarian objection, but an objection of reason and principle. I cannot, therefore, wonder that a man of such weight and learning as Mr. Hallam should have stood aloof from the party to which he was politically attached, and should have said that he could not discern in their measure the principles which he had studied and had done so much to illustrate. And yet, can a measure be lightly spoken of, or hastily judged for any of these reasons, which was demanded by a nation if it was ever so much limited by the opinions and habits of a class—a measure which must have been carried in spite of the opinions and inclinations of many of those who framed and supported it—a measure which appears to have averted a revolution, if it approached the borders of one—to have saved the monarchy, if it implied another and different kind of dominion from that of any monarch —a measure which has apparently produced all those good fruits that were enumerated with so much eloquence by Mr. Lowe as arguments against any further reform? It seems to me that in this sense the bill has a basis in the history of our land, and affirms, not contradicts, the lessons of that history. The most organic class in the country—that which felt itself to be organic, was able to assert for itself a place in the national order. No inorganic body has done that, or has ever had the least capacity for doing it. The enormous force which I described as coming into existence during the last century, as receiving its direction and form from the inventions of Arkwright and Watt—this had stood aloof from the House of Commons, had been most inadequately represented in it. Yet it was one of the most compact and orderly forces in the country, and one part of it—that part which supplied the capital to great manufacturing enterprises—was *conscious* of this force; it *knew* that it was a power. A dangerous knowledge for any body, I apprehend, which looks upon itself as a separate order, having interests apart from those of the commonwealth;—a useful knowledge, if the body which possesses it can be accepted into the commonwealth, can become a living member of the commonwealth, not an excrescence upon it.

Any one who has this conception of the nature of the Reform Bill will have the pleasure of regarding its authors as benefactors to the land. He will be prepared to appreciate that particular kind of service which it is said to have rendered to England, and yet will not close his ears to the different complaints which arose against it from very opposite quarters in the years that followed the enactment of it. Through it may have come—as Mr. Lowe affirms have come—the emancipation of different trades from the fetters of restriction and encouragement, the repeal of the duties on corn, certain acts of toleration and justice to religious communities standing apart from the Established Church. I do not undervalue these services when I say that they are just such as might be expected from a tolerably enlightened middle class. I show great thankfulness for the position which it has obtained, when I contend that if it had not been admitted to a substantive place in the legislature, and to greater influence in the elections, it would have thwarted a number of those measures which it has promoted. Mr. Canning and Mr. Huskisson dreaded, I apprehend, the acquisition of power by the tradesmen and manufacturers, because they obstructed many of their schemes for free trade as being injurious to their particular interests. Would not these obstructions be greater, might not the landed interest and the manufacturing interest agree each to sustain the monopolies of the other, supposing the boroughs, which often sent up clever men superior to the prejudices of both, were possessed by the burgher class? It has proved to be a false calculation, though a very natural one. The burgher class, having a voice in the legislature, has abandoned many of the narrow notions which it had when it was apart from the legislature; it has forced the landed class to abandon many of theirs.

All this is true. But was it not also true—as the most intelligent men felt and said after the passing of the Reform Bill—that there was a dead money weight upon the thought and energies of the land which it must contrive to shake off, or it would lose its freedom and manliness? Was there no logic in the cry of the lowest class, that if the principle of number was that which determined the representation, their exclusion was anomalous and monstrous? There was the ready answer to the first: "You are not practical; your notions smell of a mediæval period, or else of some fantastic millennium to come hereafter." There was the ready answer to the second; "Numbers without property can only lead to anarchy." Each answer had its weight. Each acted upon the class to which it was *not* addressed. The intellectual men dreaded the invasion of the mob. The multitude regarded the intellectual men as the natural allies of the aristocracy. The moneyed class could keep them at a distance from each other, if it could not reconcile either to itself. It could exercise a similar influence on the religious instincts which were at work in the land. It disliked the enthusiasm of Churchmen and Dissenters, of Roman Catholics and Protestants. It could not actually quench the enthusiasm of any, or prevent it from often passing into fanaticism. But it could keep each apart from the other; it could create perpetual suspicions and jealousies of each in the other.

But the year 1848 came. The middle-class domination in France collapsed. The under strata of society again discovered the power that was latent in them. How different the cries were in this revolution from those in the first, must be perceived by every thoughtful man. *Then* it was the shout for natural and individual rights; *now* it was the demand for the organization of labour;—a difference of the most pregnant kind, affecting, I conceive, all the after-history of other countries as well as of France. But the difference was not perceived by the Chartists, who thought of reproducing the movement in England. Some visions they had of organization; but the force of mere numbers, of an aggregation of units, was that which they were most inclined to set against the forces which they saw were chiefly recognised in England. The impotence of mere numbers in the face of organization was soon painfully made known to them. The army was composed of units, but the smallest troop had that in it which was wanting to their millions. Whether their discomfiture, whether the insanity of their monster petition, is an argument for keeping the classes to which they belonged inorganic, or for leading them to seek organization, and, through that, the full responsibilities of citizenship, is a question which may occupy us hereafter. With that question another may arise; whether it is not possible that the intellectual objections to the Reform Bill of 1831, and the objections which have had most influence with the members of the working class, may both be removed if we recur to those principles of the constitution which both are wont to regard as narrow and obsolete; whether they may not provide the fullest recognition of the positive dignity of the middle class without permitting it to become the tyrant over any other?

Let me say here, in reference to the special subject of this chapter, that I do not anticipate any satisfactory issue of this inquiry, unless full justice be done to that phrase "sovereignty of the people," which the first French Revolution has bequeathed to us. *Full justice*, which does not mean in this case, any more than in the case of the rights of man, or education according to nature, an acceptance of the phrase unsifted and untested, in the sense which was given to it by those who first used it. They cast forth a maxim on the world which was to prove what was in it by a series of experiments; so that at last the kernel might be saved and the husk might be cast away. Whatever involves the worship of Demus as of a divine monarch who may decree what he likes, may put down one and set up another, dealing with all as his tools to execute his commands, I repudiate as a husk, hard, coarse, and tough, but not substantial. Whoever flatters a mob—I would say this emphatically on the eve of a general election—does not reverence a people, does not love them, but hates them or despises them. With this flattery I would join the boast of conforming to the will of a majority. So help me God, I do not mean to follow the will of a majority, I hope never to follow it, always to set it at nought. And for that expression about "the greatest happiness of the greatest number," I do not understand it. I have no measure of it. I cannot tell what happiness is, or how it is to be distributed among the greatest number, or how the greatest number is to be ascertained. If it could be put to the vote of the greatest number what they would have for happiness, I have no security that they would not decide for something profoundly low and swinish.

But I do find a kernel within this husk, and a very precious kernel. The chief of all is said, on authority which I deem sacred, to be the servant of all. It was a truth asserted in a thousand phrases and forms by kings and popes at the time of the French Revolution. But it was practically denied by kings and popes. Who should be above others; who should *not* acknowledge a service; this *was* the struggle. I cannot deny that it *is* the struggle still; that we are all competing for prizes, that we are all impatient of service, even when we beg for it. Yet I trust there is a growing sense in sovereigns, in nobles, in all officials, that they are to be servants of the people. If servants they cannot be slaves; they must think and act as freemen; they cannot perform their duties on any other terms. If servants of a people, they must consider other days as well as their own; what is due to the past, what is due to the future. To give the men of our own day the sense that they belong to a people, that they have an inheritance from the past and in the future; this must be the work of our education. If any aspire to be our representatives, they must carry with them the same conviction. If they think only for the present, if they legislate only for the present, the interests of the present will be sacrificed. In forgetting our forefathers, they will forget us; in cheating our children, they will cheat us.

CHAPTER VII.

MANHOOD SUFFRAGE AND MONEY SUFFRAGE.

IT seemed to the Chartists, in 1848 and 1849, as if their demands had been merely put down by force. Were they not fair deductions from the principle of the Reform Bill? " You have acknowledged that boroughs are to be disfranchised which have not a certain number of inhabitants. You have acknowledged that towns are to be enfranchised which have a certain number of inhabitants. Is not number, then, the ground of representation, according to your own showing?" The champions of the bill could answer, " No! that was not our standard; if it had been, we should not have fixed the £50 qualification for counties, the £10 for towns." "True," was the Chartists' response, "you did not mean what you seemed to mean. But we did. You were glad of our help to cry for the bill and the whole bill. Now we want you to determine to which rule you will adhere. Avow one principle or the other. Say the

House of Commons represents the possessors of land and money; or say it represents the body of the people. If the last, you must accept our charter".

I may not have put the arguments of the Chartists exactly as they were put by their advocates. But this, I think, was the dilemma in which they strove to involve, and did involve, their friends of the middle classes who had worked with them in 1831. I do not see any escape from this dilemma, for those who thought they could ascertain who constitute the *people* of any country, by taking the sum of its inhabitants. And that, as I have said already, had become the prevalent opinion among those who most directed the judgment of the ten-pound householders. It may be questioned whether their representatives in the House of Commons would not, in general, have treated any other conception of a people as fantastic and absurd. They were therefore deliberately endowing a small section of the people with privileges which by their own theory of the constitution belonged to a larger.

But if the numerical doctrine was accepted in terms, resisted in fact, by those who clung to the Reform Bill of 1831, it was rejected in fact, though it was retained in terms, by those who sympathised most heartily with the French Revolution of 1848. The *ouvriers* of Paris practically disclaimed the notion that number was the secret of power. We must, they said, have an organization of labour; we are nothing without that. An expression, I think, of a great truth, whatever errors might be mixed with their apprehensions of it; of a truth which would in due time become very intelligible to Englishmen of all classes. The middle class had no real faith in units. The merchants formed companies and partnerships; so they exhibited their strength. A hundred Englishmen, or less than a hundred, went forth to found a colony. They felt themselves a people. 50,000 or 500,000 savages might be about them; these they felt were not a people. The labourers, in like manner, recognising organization to be their necessity, were abjuring the faith in units. They were adopting the same idea of a people as that which had been implied in all the social life which was already established.

I have thus been brought back to the principle from which I started. Every step in our history which we have been considering, has illustrated and confirmed it. We have been tracing the growth of a people; there was a living, however tiny, seed of order; this the rains and the sun nurtured; it had all possible obstructions when it came above the surface and began to send forth shoots. But it became stronger for all the influences which threatened to kill it, expanded in the air, became sickly under every attempt to confine it in hothouses. Here is life; here is the promise of ever-fresh development. Introduce the miserable theory of numbers, and you have nothing but a series of plots and counterplots : plots to gain admission into a narrow, exclusive circle; counterplots to keep the circle more narrow, to devise precautions against intruders. Thence arise perpetual suspicions of the few against the many, and of the many against the few; of the few against each other, of each one in the many against his neighbours; ending in the domination of one who reduces all to the condition of corpses, and then boasts that by destroying freedom he has secured equality.

If we apply these lessons to the questions which are agitating England now—which will undergo a discussion at every one of the coming elections, and will certainly be brought before the next Parliament —we may clear away some confusions, at least from our own minds. I am not about to propose any new theory or scheme of representation. I think we have quite enough of theories. I do not say we have *too many*, because each, I doubt not, has something in it which is not in any other, and which may contribute to a practical result. But I shall not add one to the list. I would only inquire whether there is not an old doctrine which we have somewhat lost sight of in our pursuit of novelties; whether we cannot recover it; whether, if we do, we may not turn all recent suggestions to better account.

Two demands have survived the Chartist movement; one is described as the demand for manhood suffrage, the other for universal suffrage. The phrases are often supposed to be identical by their opponents; perhaps they often appear identical to the persons who use them. Yet they express very different instincts; if followed out, they would produce very different effects. Listen carefully to the statements and arguments of any one who pleads for manhood suffrage. You will see that he means to protest against the notion that a certain amount of capital, great or small, determines the worth of a man, or his qualification for being a citizen. That anything which a man has should be set above that which he is, shocks the objector's conscience. He deems it an immoral inversion; he sees in it the root of meanness and injustice. I never could discourage this kind of feeling. I should think that I was injuring a neighbour's soul, and injuring my own, if I used any arguments, however plausible, which could diminish in him the sense of the preciousness of manhood, or which could lead him for a moment to measure the preciousness of money against it. The best argument I could employ would be this, that a man who has earned a competence, who is able to live without depending on the bounty of others, has given a test of his manhood; that he has shown himself capable of self-restraint, and of patient toil. There is much weight in that statement. I would gladly lead a capitalist to dwell upon it, and to recollect that his worth lies not in his capital, only in that which it indicates. If he brought five shillings to London, and has become a millionaire, let him have all the honour of his conflict with poverty, and his endurance of it. And let him esteem that his main honour. For the rewards which the struggle has produced he is responsible. But if he tries to make the value of them a part of *his* value, he posts his books wrongly, the ledger must be submitted to a more careful accountant. Therefore I should be afraid to press this argument far, if I were conversing with a mechanic. I do not want him to envy the millionaire. I do not want him to think that he has less an interest in the wellbeing of his country than the millionaire. I do not believe that he has. I count it an unsafe thing that he should hold that opinion. Therefore, I will take no pains to discourage him when he defends manhood suffrage on this plea; I will rather try to encourage him in fully considering the signification of his own words, in determining not to part with them.

But if I saw that by manhood suffrage he understood universal suffrage, I should then ask to enter into explanations with him. I should not run a tilt against the phrase as if I thought it expressed a vague fanatical dream. I should not show the least fear of it, as if it pointed to a result which might endanger the stability of some class in which I was interested. I do not reckon it a dream to desire that all who dwell in a land should, in the fullest sense, be citizens of that land. I do not know that universal suffrage if granted to-morrow might displace any class in which I am interested. One of that class, whatever it be, might, by fair or foul means, get an ascendency over the voters. They might follow him blindly. He might make them do just what he deemed most for the advantage of his class. It is just on this ground that I should reason with my friend who is disposed to identify manhood suffrage with universal suffrage. "Is that blind following a leader, say of my class or any other, what you mean by manhood? May it not become the greatest idolatry of that which is *not* manhood—of that very money which you set in contrast to manhood? What you want," I should say, "if I understand you right, is to get first the greatest quantity of manliness and wisdom—of really free judgment—in the voters; and next, so far as you can, to give each one of them an opportunity of expressing his judgment, *his* conviction. You would aim, if possible, at both these objects. You would keep the second subordinate to the first. Now, if you raise the cry for universal suffrage, you run the hazard, it seems to me, of losing both. I like your phrase, I confess, better than some which are often substituted for it, and are considered more moderate. I like it better than any talk about the 'will of the majority.' It comes nearer to my desire that the majority should *not* prevail—that those who do not think with the majority should have an opportunity of signifying what they think. But by talking of general suffrage or universal suffrage, you will only promote the slavish reverence for numbers, and with it the dominion of some person who can turn numbers his own way—a noble, it may be—a millionaire, a priest, a demagogue; you will get your thousands or ten thousands of votes, but their value will be nothing, except what they derive from the unit which goes before them. Now, such a suffrage, I say, is not worth the search of any set of serious or intelligent men. It will not express their serious or intelligent purpose as a body. It will not denote the serious or intelligent conviction of the distinct men who compose the body."

Suppose, then, we did set this object deliberately before us; to get the greatest amount of manhood possible in the electors (we will waive the question which has been raised by Mr. Mill, whether under that name we are to include womanhood, though it is worthy of all consideration), how may we hope for any solution of the problem? What I maintain is, that history has in great part solved it for us, and that earnest reflection upon the circumstances of our time, upon the steps that have been actually taken, upon the wishes that are strongest and the energies that are most awake in the land, may complete the solution of it. The hindrances to the attainment of a practical result are not to be dissembled. They arise from good feelings as well as bad, in all the classes of the land; from genuine faith, as well as from unworthy distrust; from a perception of real dangers, as well as from cowardly dread of imaginary dangers. But they may be overcome; nothing will help to overcome them so much, as a steady examination of them.

You may remember the word which I quoted from a speech of Coriolanus in Shakespeare, and which I said described very admirably the feelings of a patrician of his class respecting the plebeians. He regarded them as fragments. He did not like to see them acquiring the solidity, the coherency which belonged to his own order. He saw that if they did acquire it, the senate's concession to them of a set of tribunes must be confirmed, and must be followed by more concessions of the like kind. Well; this contempt for fragments in an organic society was, I thought, very natural; fragments cannot be respected as such. We respect them, when we think they have the capacity for being something else than fragments. In every stage of our own history, the class which has been within the circle of the people or the citizens has shown a desire that those who lay without it might be kept in the fragmentary condition. There was this desire at the time when Leicester summoned the freeholders and the freemen to send representatives to Parliament. But it could not prevail. The freeholders had asserted a distinct position. They were not dependent on the great lords of the soil; they held only of the King. They had attained their manhood. It must be recognised. The freemen of the towns had served their apprenticeship, and entered into guilds, had exercised municipal functions; they had attained their manhood. They must be adopted as regular members of the commonwealth. The freeholders had their forty shillings, no doubt. The freemen might perhaps be householders. But in each case it was not the money qualification which designated them for their new duties. It was that which their name expressed. They had passed through a stage of discipline. They had become emancipated. They had capacities for serving their own neighbourhood, their own town; serving it as slaves could not serve it. They had capacities for serving the country at large. The King must claim their services for it. He did claim them as we have seen. If the House of Commons was the fruit of a revolution, the legitimate monarch maintained the institution. He tried to make it merely his instrument for raising taxes. He tried to make the position of its members a disagreeable one. Agreeable or disagreeable, it became a mighty one. It upheld the national feeling against the foreign ecclesiastical feeling. It worked with the King in securing the Reformation. It worked against the King when he tried to be absolute. It fell when it tried to be absolute itself. After it had begun to work harmoniously with the Crown, it sank into corruption, the whole land felt the weakness which came from that corruption. The question how to deliver it from its corruption became one which able ministers of the last century saw they must try to settle. They could not settle it. There was a new power rising in the country, the great manufacturing power which they could not take account of; till it was taken account of, there could be no parliamentary reform. That power had organised itself in our century. In 1831, it compelled a recognition of itself. Because it was so mighty and coherent, the Reform Bill, though introduced by members of the aristocracy, was in fact its bill.

What next? That part of the manufacturing body who are not capitalists, who are simply workmen, have also exhibited a longing to be organised. Those who are capitalists have exhibited the same disinclination to gratify that longing which the English patricians exhibited when their class established itself in guilds and corporations, and then became represented in the legislature. Nevertheless, it has been accomplishing itself by degrees. First, the experiment took a mere negative form, the form of antagonism to capital. Thence trade unions, which are so great a power in the land, had mainly their origin —though positive self-government, sometimes of a beneficial, sometimes of a hurtful kind, mingled with their strikes and their denunciations of employers. When the laws against the combination of workmen were taken off, these bodies, being less secret, being open to observation from without, became far less dangerous and oppressive than they had been. Still they were in a normal attitude of hostility to another class. After 1848 the dread of organized labour became stronger in the middle class. " It must lead to a revolution like the French." But it diffused itself further and further, especially in the north of England. The legislature was wise enough to withdraw the restraints which it had imposed on the partnerships of workmen. Associations, formed not for resistance to capitalists, but for positive objects— for the production and exchange of goods—became numerous. When these bodies were patronised by the higher classes, they generally failed. Those which arose from the spontaneous efforts of the workmen have succeeded beyond all the expectations of their most sanguine members. They have borne the shock of the cotton famine. Fifteen years ago both our great reviews held them up to suspicion—the one, as being hostile to the maxims of political economy; the other, as smelling of democracy. Within the last year and a half both these reviews have expressed the greatest admiration of them—the one, because they exhibit the soundest adherence to the maxims of political economy; the other, because they have such an essentially conservative character.

Now, it would certainly appear as if this were a development of national life in the country pointing in the same direction as that which led to the summoning of freemen to Parliament in the days of Henry III. Here you have bodies of men giving precisely the same tests of capacity for management of affairs, for internal government, which the men of the town gave at that time. There may be many confusions in their proceedings, as there were in those of their predecessors, but they compel us to acknowledge that what we have to dread is inorganic multitudes; that which we have earnestly to desire is that every part of that which we call, and must call, *the community*, should be delivered from that disorder.

To this conclusion the arguments of Mr. Lowe, of which I spoke in the last chapter, evidently point. He made the House laugh, and at the same time tremble, by quoting passages from the celebrated Feargus O'Connor petition, advocating that system of regulating wages and profits which had yielded with such difficulty to the facts and reasonings of free-traders; advocating also the abolition of the national debt, of the House of Lords, of the Established Church, &c. He dwelt on the numbers who signed this petition. Admit their right in virtue of their multitude to vote, and they must swamp all the other classes in the country; they must destroy its institutions and its honesty. Exactly; and they may work this mischief though you do not admit them to vote. A mere multitude must be dangerous. It must be ready to adopt the opinions of any leader who obtains temporary dominion over it, let them be as wild as they may. *Any* multitude will do this—a well-dressed one, a learned one, no less than one in rags. And if you could induce any portion of those multitudes—the well-dressed, the learned, or the ragged — to feel that it had a position, a moral responsibility, that it belonged to an order, the notions which it had adopted in blind submission to some foolish guide would be at once renounced or silently forgotten. If so, should we not hail any rise of actual societies of men out of this incoherent mass? Will not such societies, engaged in actual business, feeling that they have responsibilities and a place to maintain, be our best protectors against these destructive dogmas? Should not we desire to include them in the commonwealth, to make them know that they are members of it?

(2.) Looking at the subject from this point of view, I do not feel quite able to understand the views of those who opposed, or of those who supported the bill of Mr. Baines, for reducing the qualification for the franchise in towns from ten pounds to six pounds. As to the first, though we may attribute very great wisdom to the framers of the Reform Bill of 1831, we cannot quite give them credit for a divination which should have discovered the precise fraction of revenue which makes an elector safe and worthy to be trusted, and less than which makes him dangerous. Mr. Lowe supposes Lord Grey and Lord Russell to have been endowed with this miraculous gift, since he attributes all conceivable blessings to a measure which settled the franchise at ten pounds, and foretells evils unspeakable from the descent to six. On the other hand, I would ask the champions of that measure, whether they are not deluding themselves in supposing that they approach one step nearer to those who exalt a manhood above a money franchise, by reducing the money scale? The objection, rightly understood, is to the principle of such a franchise, which the new bill would perpetuate. No doubt there is wisdom in preserving this continuity of legislation. But to run exactly in the groove of a bill just thirty years old, *may* not be the best means of preserving that continuity. I have two reasons for thinking that it *would* not be the best means. The first is, that the Reform Bill itself broke through the continuity of legislation by substituting the fifty pound and the ten pound franchise for the old distinctions of the freeholder and the freeman. If we try to revive this distinction, we cannot be accused of deserting the line in which our predecessors have travelled. The second reason is, that we shall unfold the principle of the Reform Bill, which recognised one part of the manufacturing force of the country (that which was embodied in the holders of manufacturing capital) as requiring to be represented, if we now recognise the other part of it, the working members of it, as having duties to the land which they confess they cannot fulfil unless they also have the obligation of choosing representatives.

(3.) I call it an *obligation*, rather than a privilege or a right, two names about the value of which there has been a dispute. In doing so, I encounter what was by far the most powerful and telling argument in Mr. Lowe's celebrated speech. He denied that there was any eager desire for the franchise in those who did not possess it. Many, he said, could obtain, it at a very slight sacrifice, and they did not care to make that sacrifice. I have no doubt that Mr. Lowe had the clearest and most satisfactory data for this assertion. I believe it might have been carried further. I am convinced that very many working men actually *decline* the franchise when they might have it without any sacrifice at all. Not a few may take pains to avoid it, calculating that the exercise of it may bring them into trouble with men of the class above them, whose candidate they refuse. Not a few may shrink from the temptation to which a privilege, notoriously so often abused, may expose them. Among these recusants, therefore, there may be many estimable people most advantageously contrasted with others who reckon their votes a commodity which can be turned to profit. I think this statement applies to working men, but not at all exclusively. It is the same with many, perhaps as many, of the shopkeepers. It is the same with not a few of the professional class, and with not a few men of letters.

Do I treat this fact as one of slight importance? No; it seems to me one of the greatest importance; full of sad and serious warning to all the land, indicating a state of mind which must be corrected, which we should use all our energies to correct. It is one of many indications of a listlessness and apathy about public affairs which cannot be safe. It is one of the proofs that some new blood requires to be poured into the commonwealth, some hearty zeal for its interests. Where are you to find this? Not in a set of six-pound householders, Mr. Lowe affirms. But his statement goes beyond that. It applies to the present franchise, whatever weight it may have in our judgment of the future. The ten-pound householders show that *they* do not prize the gift you have bestowed on them. Why should they? What bond is there between men because they pay the same rent to different landlords? What is there in that fact to inspire them with any common interest or feelings? What is there in it to bring forth the feeling in each man that he is a citizen, that he owes something to the country? Where there is no fellowship there will be no sense of individual responsibility; and, therefore, what is coming to pass in your House of Commons? You have, and will have, various interests represented there. The ten-pound householder will vote for this railway director, for that great shipowner. They will vote for him because he gives them a motive to vote for him; it may be a respectable, it may be a discreditable one. But they have no interest of their own, nothing which makes them a substantive body in society; nothing which can make them understand why they should be represented, or what there is in them which can be represented. The price which they pay for their tenement does not create any of those instincts which belong to a society of freemen. They may have those instincts; for they may be members of some religious congregation, of some club or trade union. They

CARE FOR MINORITIES. 221

may have the true sacred sense of citizenship—the sense of being fathers, husbands, brothers. But the ten pound or six pound has nothing to do with any of these sympathies. That suggests nothing but what is disagreeable. The Franchise is an additional burthen on the rent; the tenant must decide which of two sets of persons whom he wishes to please he will offend.

All traditions, then, of the past, all the circumstances of the present time, all the confessions and arguments of clever men who have opposed reform, suggest that the pecuniary standard and the numerical are equally unsatisfactory methods of ascertaining where the strength of a people is, and whence it should be recruited. Various symptoms show that the most intelligent and patriotic men are becoming awake to this conviction. The co-operative movement, where it has been vigorous, has proceeded from the workers themselves. But there is another movement in which they have cordially accepted the help of other classes, and have submitted themselves to their guidance. No greater sign of the new heart which is imparted to all classes of a nation, when they can work for a common object, no greater proof of the blessings and rewards of mutual confidence, has ever been seen than the rise and progress of our Volunteers. All now feel it to be so. Yet it had at its outset to endure plentiful ridicule. Most sagacious men doubted whether it was possible to get men, with no evident personal interest, to endure the weariness and humiliation of drill. Many declared that the whole effort was the result of a temporary panic; many questioned whether there was any national spirit left among us which could respond to such an appeal. These doubts have been generally quelled; we have confessed that there is a sense of order, and a desire for order, among all classes of our people, and that the order is associated with thoughts of life and freedom. Surely the lessons are not exhausted yet. Is there not a security in bodies like these for an honest choice, for a choice which shall be determined by conviction, not bribes, such as no money tests can give? Is there not a will and a purpose in them which more deserves to be represented than the will of a mere majority ever can?

Most thankful also should we be for the various signs which are afforded by recent schemes that this phrase is losing the magical attraction which it once had for political reasoners; that it can no longer be the watchword which it was thirty years ago. All the most ingenious devices of our day are to provide some way in which minorities may express their sentiments, or to create particular franchises which may give men, not able to make their voices heard in a crowd, a chance of manifesting convictions which the country cannot afford to lose. I value all such suggestions as the token of a change which is at work among us—of a willingness to undergo trouble for the sake of ascertaining what there is among us which *can* be represented, not to acquiesce in certain rough and ready standards, which are easy enough to find, and are worthless when they are found. But I can understand the suspicions and protests which these ingenious arrangements awaken. There is, to say the least, much awkwardness in first framing a general scheme, and then considering what measures you can take to counteract the effects of it. But there is more than awkwardness. Those whom you enfranchise by your general measure, will suppose that you have only adopted them because you are afraid of them; that you do not want them; that you know they will be about some mischief which you must try to neutralise. If your object is to make a concession to a certain class, you cannot do it more ungraciously. But if you have no business to think about concessions to any class, if your only duty is to provide the constitution which is best for the whole land—then all notion of devices to enfeeble any part of the representation should be cast aside; you should wish each part of it to be as strong as it can be.

I do not call these schemes *crotchetty*. That is a vulgar epithet which may be used against the best plans or the worst, which often denotes only the laziness of the man who resorts to it. Nor do I doubt that their propounders have a hearty desire to secure an efficient representation for the country. But I think they have been misled partly by the vehemence with which some able men still plead for the will of a majority as the standard of truth; partly by certain habits which belong to a money-getting race; partly by what I must call the effeminacy of those who belong to the intellectual or literary class. I will say a word or two on each of these points.

The worshippers of majorities often appeal to the United States; I believe they could not choose a more unfortunate instance for their purpose. Take their history at any point you please. Did the New England colonists go forth to assert the will of a majority, or to exhibit the strength which lies in a small, persecuted minority actuated by a strong conviction? Did the colonies grow up as majorities, or as little bodies, surrounded by an incoherent mass, which some of them thought they might slaughter, which some of them tried to civilize? Did they conquer the mother country by majorities, or by the little force which Washington's calm and steady sense—hampered continually by the perverseness and want of patriotism in majorities—was able to bring into order and make efficient? Was not the great resistance in the minds of educated men to the emancipation of the slaves, the fear that the coloured majority should crush the intelligence of the whites? Was that fear and all the mighty interests which worked with it, overcome at last by a majority, or by the steadfast resolution of a small minority, convinced that the intelligence and civilization of the whites were not promoted, but were certain to be extinguished, by their wrong-doings? All that has been greatest in the history of this great country from its first days to its latest, has been a witness not for, but against, the maxim which it has been used to establish. You may call the States a democracy if you mean that they are without a hereditary king, or a House of Lords. But Jefferson, who pompously announced the sovereignty of the people, and the equality of men, was a slaveholder. Lincoln, who broke the chains of the slave, affirmed in the speech at his inauguration the great truth which he sealed by his death—that the people is not its own ruler— that there is a righteous Ruler over it, who calls it to account for its oppressions and sins, and whose righteousness it must confess, if it would not perish. Such a declaration was much more than the sentiment of a devout and humble man impressed with the awful responsibility of his own position and of his country's position. It linked the old idea of freedom in the New England Puritan, the freedom of him whom God has raised out of his natural slavery, with the later reverence for the man as man, without respect of race or colour. It took away from the first idea its exclusiveness—from the second the vagueness which might easily sink into carelessness about the strength of manhood, the degradation of mere animal existence. If America enters into the principle of her great chief, the problem which now agitates her about negro suffrage will not be solved by any pedantic adherence to the rule that all her inhabitants must elect those who are to legislate for them, nor yet by a prejudice about blood. How the fullest expression of the free mind of its citizens can be secured—how the deepest moral convictions of the land can be secured—will be the only question, a question upon which Englishmen must be utterly unable to pronounce, but which they may rejoice if their own annals should afford any help in settling. The balance of instruction will be still much in our favour. If our English workmen remember the words of that admirable man of their own order to which I have referred, they may restore the faith in an actual Lord of the nation to us who are fast losing it. I know no class which has so much interest in *not* exalting the majority into His throne.

Whilst any rag of that worship cleaves to our minds, we must look out for some inventions, clever or clumsy, to avert the practical inconvenience of it. But there is another worship which threatens us, that which, in our sneers at a people who have made a grand effort for five years to shake it off, we used to call the worship of the Dollar. That various moneyed interests should get themselves represented in Parliament, is not only inevitable, it is most desirable. These interests have proved themselves to be a power in the land. Every such power ought to have an expression. But the prevalent notion is, that we can have nothing but these interests, nothing but a perpetual balance of one against the other. What can the legislation be which is the result of a mere competition and collision between the self-seeking of different companies and capitalists? No wonder if many men as radical as Cobbett—much less swayed by impulse than he was—should exclaim with him, " Thank God, we have a House of Lords !" Any one who regards that House as a witness for the sacredness of family life, for a continuous national history, may join in that thanksgiving—may desire that the Upper House should maintain its own position, and should never seek to exercise a dishonourable influence over the elections for the Lower House. But surely this House cannot be a sufficient protection against the conflicting force of trading interests. Hereditary property may become mixed with them, even dependent upon them. May there not be some element in the nation which is national, and which might assist in turning partial sympathies, even partial antipathies, to the service of the whole land ? Such an element, if it exists at all, can scarcely be sought for amongst capitalists. If it has not yet been found among workmen, may not that be owing to the fact that capitalists have not *wished* them to be united—have rather liked that there should be as many separate interests amongst them as among themselves ? Shall not those who care for the intelligence, the dignity, the unity of the land, cherish the opposite desire ? Are not these in danger, from the want of some unmoneyed class to sustain them ?

I press this consideration upon that dainty and delicate order called the intellectual or the literary one, which has an extraordinary reverence for itself and its own powers, and yet has, with that, a strange dread, lest those who are without any of these powers should subvert and extinguish it. Persons of this class are often eager to find some security, that if the working men are allowed an increased share in the representation, they also may obtain an increased share of it; so there will be a counterpoise to what they suppose must be a weight of uncultivated, semi-barbarous opinion. That they should covet an opportunity of taking part in public affairs, that they should be stimulated to do so by almost any motive, is a good thing. For their temptation is to stand aloof from affairs, to overlook them with a lofty and serene pity, just to notice them for the purpose of pointing out the absurdity of all parties that are occupied with them. But I cannot admit that the reason which they give for suddenly assuming the rights of citizens, and desiring to have them in a larger measure, is a valid or a creditable one. We *do* want the protection of earnest intelligent thinkers against what is called, falsely called, practical common sense. We do want it, because that which assumes the name of common sense is not common, but partial and narrow; because that which calls itself practical is often the attempt to work out some ill-digested theory, which cannot be worked out except to the injury of all who meddle with it. But do not our wise men find this bad counterfeit of a precious quality active in the House of Commons, and among the constituencies *now?* Does not the power of it lie in the notions about money and money's worth which prevail in both? Is it not a very ignominious notion for men of letters to entertain, that a constituency not representing money would be their great antagonist? If it is so, I am afraid literature itself must be passing into a trade which clings chiefly to money for its support, which dreams of little beyond the market or what can be procured in the market. Whether this epicurism takes a gross or a refined shape, whether it seeks its patrons among the nobles or the shopkeepers, it must grow feebler, more merely sensational or more merely scornful every day. Those who cultivate this temper will be trodden under foot by some race of hardy Goths, some stout sons of the soil. Would it not be better if they tried to renovate their strength by communion with those sons of the soil? Might they not get much from them and impart something to them?

I shall have more to say on this subject before I conclude. I notice it now, because it bears upon a scheme which I once thought very plausible, for introducing into the legislature a set of men who should expressly represent those who are engaged in pursuits of a more or less decidedly literary character. I do not say that no modification of such a scheme may be possible or desirable; but I confess to having become more doubtful of the expediency of investing men of letters with the character of a separate caste, as I have become more convinced of the duties which they owe to the rest of their countrymen, and of the blessings which they may receive if they do not prefer their magnificence to the performance of these duties. I feel, however, much gratitude to the propounders of every such scheme. All any of us can hope, is to contribute some element to the consideration of the subject, to throw some seed into the ground which may germinate hereafter. This hint is of great value, inasmuch as it puts us upon seeking in what way we may get the greatest amount of intelligence into our representation. It may not, perhaps, be contributed in its largest share by the classes which make intellect their profession. They may be liable to some conceits and affectations. They may choose candidates who embody certain conceptions of theirs; men with little thought, with very feeble purposes, because so many different fancies have to be consulted, and the compromise between them may be a most unsatisfactory one. Intellect which should be robust, may under such treatment become lean and fantastical. That which should be original, may become conventional. Still it is good to be reminded that in a House of Commons, wisdom is wanted more than fine gold.

Still more important and free from the objection to which this project is open, is the skilful and laborious contrivance of Mr. Hare, for giving every person in the country an opportunity of expressing a judgment, if he has one, in favour of some candidate. When I use the word laborious, I mean to describe only the great pains and industry which must have preceded the invention of such a plan, not the least to intimate, that it would cause labour to those who should endeavour to act upon it. Men who have examined it most carefully, and have the best right to give an opinion, are confident that it would be found easy and simple in its operation. If I do not enlarge upon it here, it is not in the least because I am insensible to the interest of the subject, or because I affect to think lightly of it as being mechanical. Every good machine involves a principle; I do not see how a principle can ever come into operation without a machinery. I only leave this scheme in other hands, because they are more competent to deal with it, and because the business that I have proposed to myself is one of a different kind. The influence of education upon representation is that which I have undertaken to consider. With some remarks upon that topic, I shall gather up the lessons which I have been trying to discover in our history.

I have given the supporters of manhood suffrage credit for two objects. First, they would seek to get the manhood of the community represented in Parliament; secondly, they would as far as possible get the sentiments of each man represented in it. I assumed that as wise men they would postpone the second of these objects to the first, though they would not willingly lose sight of either. I do not advocate this postponement because I think that the opinion of a society is worth more than the opinion of an individual. That may not be true; the reverse of it may be true. But I mean that the individual man never has play for his thoughts and faculties except he is in a society; that he is most of an individual when he is most in association and communion with other men—when he feels most his dependence upon them and his obligations to them. For the sake, then, of obtaining as much as ever we can of individual manhood, I would first turn to bodies of men, I would seek for the expression of their beliefs in the legislature. It is for this reason that I have spoken in this chapter of co-operative societies and Volunteer corps. It is for this reason that I have wished to turn the thoughts of those who are occupied with the reform of the House of Commons especially in this direction. Then their skill in devising franchises merely to counteract the pressure of a majority will not be called for. If they seek for the organic portion of the working classes, in these they will find the best and most effectual guarantees against any mere mob dictation; much more effectual than we can get from a pecuniary limitation of the franchise. The working classes themselves will find their belief on the subjects which most especially concern them, far more thoroughly and satisfactorily expressed through these agencies than they could be if ever so many loose and floating units were added to their number. A whole set of questions which are now most imperfectly handled in the House of Commons —handled by men looking at them from a distance— seeing them from their own points of view—unable to sympathise with the labourers if they wish it ever so much—would then be submitted to fair and reasonable discussion. These representatives of the workers would have no preponderance, but they would have a fair hearing—a power of stating their wishes and originating measures which they have felt to be desirable. And Mr. Lowe's testimony to the benefits which the country at large has derived from the special middle-class influence during the last thirty years, in adjusting the strife between land and trade —between the dogmas of economists and the interests of both—may be expanded thirty years hence into a testimony to the immense blessings which the working-class power has procured in the adjustment of that quarrel between labour and capital which is still besetting us.

But to attain this blessing, I believe the working classes ought to strive, and that we ought to strive, with them, for a higher one. They may not only help to adjust claims in which they themselves are interested; they may give a more national, more unselfish tone to the rest of society if only the better thoughts which are struggling in them can be evoked against the lower, debasing, grovelling tendencies which are assuredly struggling in them also. If we consider what kind of effort must have gone to the formation of the co-operative societies, what amount of endurance to the Lancashire distress, what national sympathy to the Volunteer movement, what freedom from the narrowness of John Bullism to the reception of Garibaldi last year—we may understand that there is in this portion of our countrymen something from which we may all derive a wholesome example and a manly impulse. If we remember how much more faith they showed than any of us showed, in the result of the American struggle, only because they believed it was the struggle of right against wrong, of freedom against slavery; though they had much greater cause than any of us to complain of its effects, and to be angry with those who persevered in it; we may feel some humiliation when we assume to be their teachers or prophets. And yet, there is no doubt that it would be sheer cowardice and base affectation to pretend that we have not a knowledge which we can impart to them and for which they would be the better. To find what it is and how it is to be imparted, is extremely difficult. A series of mistakes may be the only way of learning the secret; yet, assuredly, it is to be learnt in that way or some other.

This at least we may conclude, that no education which overlooks facts, however grand may be its designs—however well selected its instruments—can be good for anything. Those who undertook the task of teaching the working classes in our day started from this conviction. They began with the facts about the world which had been ascertained by science; these they set forth in careful treatises or able lectures. It was a wholesome course, I think. Their readers were beset with a number of notions upon a variety of subjects; to be assured that there were truths which had been discovered, and in which they might fully believe, was a great strength to the minds of those who were awake to receive the assurance. It was a noble thing to claim the universe in which we dwell as a common possession for the poor and the rich man; to affirm that its laws bind both, and may be made known to both. If some of the experiments by which these facts and laws have been ascertained could be added to the bare statement of them, what a training was this to the perception of the method which our minds follow in arriving at knowledge! What a revelation must Euclid's Elements be to many a man who is busy with rules and measures, that there is a measure for the earth as well as for every chair and table within it, that the same principles apply to both! What an illumination it may be to find that the numbers with which he deals in his common transactions have a relation to each other and obey eternal laws!

Such studies may be exceedingly profitable. Can it be less profitable that a man's eyes should be open by the practice of Drawing to the sense of the objects themselves which the lines confine, that his ears and heart should be opened by Music to an apprehension of the harmonies which are all about us for the peasant and the peer?

But there are in addition certain facts implied in the co-operative movement, the Volunteer corps, the visit of Garibaldi; the fact of men being linked by certain bonds to each other, the fact of our having a common country, which has a past as well as a present; the fact of our being bound to other countries as well as our own. We cannot pass these things by if our education is to be in facts and laws. There must be a study of the laws of association. There must be a history of the land in which we dwell; there must be some intimation of the way in which it has become interested in the well-being of foreign lands.

Then this fact of association reveals other facts less agreeable, equally needing explanation. There is a tendency to dissociate, to separate, of which each man becomes very conscious, in whatever circle he finds himself. There is a tendency in the citizens of a nation to break loose from the obligations of citizens. There is a tendency in nations to quarrel with each other. Such facts as these involve us in questions which we might be glad to avoid, but which we cannot avoid. Our experience forces them upon us. History is a comment upon that experience.

The excellent men who began the work of mechanics' institutes thought that they might leave the moral problems unconsidered and unsolved. They equally avoided political problems. If we grapple with the one we must grapple with the other. If they confront us in our own lives, they must confront the men of the working class in their lives. But especially if education has anything to do with representation—if it is desirable that men should be educated in order that they may be represented—it would be strange indeed if we confined our education to subjects of physical science, however highly we may prize it, however great the blessings may be which it confers on one class or on all classes.

The reason for that limitation we all know was this: There are various convictions—strong living convictions—in this country upon every question beyond the physical region. They clash with each other. It seemed most desirable, if it were possible, to find some subjects suggesting the thought of common fixed truths which could not be affected by the opinions of any set of men. I feel the advantage. I do not wonder at any degree of importance that was attached to it. A sense of unity and universality seems to be imparted by such an education, and what sense can be so precious as this?

But can education produce this result, or any results, by merely ignoring obvious and notorious difficulties? I believe the price which is paid for such silence is a very high one. We have seen that *organization* has had much to do with the history of our people and of its representatives. Great *convictions* have had still more to do with it. The strength in which they have existed at any given time has been the measure of the nation's strength. Their feebleness in the last century was the main cause of the feebleness of the House of Commons under the first princes of the Brunswick dynasty. They were rekindled in the heart of the people. The representative body almost unconsciously exhibited a renovated life. All the various convictions of the land have succeeded in getting themselves represented; no one has been able to stifle the other. I thank God that it is so. If interests were represented and convictions were silent, I should think the hour of our dissolution was at hand. May they all be heard; may the utterance make them more genuine and more vital! It may be true—perhaps it is—that they will not be genuine, not vital, unless there is something to bind them together; that they will become merely negative and destructive of each other. If so, the education of the workmen should be directed not to extinguish any one of the convictions which are stirring among us now, but to find some centre for them all. As a clergyman I may venture to say that I should seek that centre where President Lincoln sought it; that I should have no hope for the education of Englishmen if I did not believe that God had been educating them, and is educating them still—educating them to be in the highest sense free Englishmen and free men. I have been endeavouring in these chapters to trace the footsteps of His education. If I shall lead any man to recognise it in his own life, in the life of his country, of Christendom, of the world, he will forgive and forget the weakness of my words in the worth of lessons which every day's experience and sorrow will make more precious and wonderful to him.

INDEX.

INDEX.

ALFRED, King, the typical Saxon, and how, 24.
Anne, Queen, 143.
Arkwright and Watt, their influence on Reform, 155.
Armies, organic force of, 175.
Associations, co-operative, their bearing and influence, 215, 216.

BACON, Lord, his submission to James I., 104; consequent impoverishment of literature, 105; Bacon's merit in striking out a new path, 105.
Baines', Mr., bill and its supporters, 217; not best means of maintaining continuity of legislation, 218.
Barons, the, prove checks on royal power, 51.
Baxter's, Richard, moderation confounds parliamentary soldiers, 118.
Bentham and his disciples, 192; his vast influence here and in France, 193; two sides of his teaching, 192; his notion of government as a system of checks, 193; romantic ideas dissipated by him, 192.
Bolingbroke's, Lord, famous letter, 146.
Britons, the early, agricultural, 19.
Burdett, Sir Francis, his work, 190.
Burgher class, the, its beneficial influence on legislation, 198.
Burke, what his intercourse with Johnson proves, 149; his great mistake, the coalition ministry, 150; his Whiggism, what it bound him to, 161; his error as to the French Revolution, 163; his stern demands, 164.

CHARLES I., 108; state of his court, 110; its two enemies, 111; sorrow of Commons at his duplicity, 114; his advisers, 138.
Charles II., his advisers, 138.
Chartists, difference between' French Revolution of 1848 and first one not perceived by the, 200; their impotence in face of organization, 200; the dilemma of their friends, 204, 205.
Chaucer a citizen, his poetry unites Commons with Court, 58; Canterbury Tales assert dignity of common speech, 59; his parson a contrast to the friars, 67.
Christianity the basis of human rights, 13, 238.

Citizens, the, put forth their claims, 156.
——— aim of school to fit men for, 183; not a dream to desire all should be citizens, 209.
Citizenship, test of, in Mary's time, 91.
Clergy, the, helpers in developing freedom, 25.
——— the royalist, their tastes and tendencies, 109; their writings intolerable to the citizens, &c., 109.
Commons, the, scorned by patrician Roman, 8.
——— first summoned to Parliament, 33.
——— how demonstration of, in Mary's time, effectual, 91.
——— sympathy of, with Crown shaken in Stuarts' time, 94.
——— not the people, but its developing power, 134.
——— House of, how it became needful, 29, 36.
——— real strength of the, 55, 56; depended on what represented, 55.
——— after the Restoration, 128; lost greatness in first half of 18th century, 144; fell in trying to be absolute, 213.
Commonwealth, danger of organic bodies standing aloof from, 197.
Conquest, the Saxon, its fruits, 21.
Convictions, as well as interests, should be represented, 238; education should find centre for convictions, 238.
Co-operative Associations, their influence, 215; changed opinions of them, 215; their development similar to what made Henry enfranchise freemen, 215; they prove organization, 216.
Coverley's, Sir Roger de, chaplain a favourable specimen, 159.
Cromwell, his view of affairs, 117; foundation of his enthusiasm, 118; love for Commons' rule became no part of his creed, 120; his belief in a divine call to rule, 121; proof of this his appointing Richard successor, 122; did not wish Parliament dependent on army, 121; Carlyle's merits and errors in relation to him, 122.

DECLARATION of Right, the Whig historians do not overrate it, 132.

INDEX.

Divine right, legacy left by the idea of, 139; Sir R. Filmer's doctrine of, 139; Sir R. refuted by Locke, 140; maxims of St. John, 140; Sir Robert Walpole's notions of, 141.

Dryden, instability of the time typed in, 135; this instability clearly mirrored in Commons, 135.

EDUCATION as related to French Revolution, 181; in relation to nature, 182; new provisions needed for education of poorer classes, 184; the different courses proposed, 185; sectarian teaching, 185; possibilities of combination, 186; effects of Rousseau's Nature system, 186; Wordsworth s relation to it, 187; true idea of education, 188; it must not overlook facts, 234; its higher aim insight into general law, 236; should find centre for convictions of all, 238; God that centre, 239.

Edward I., policy of, 47; ingenious and so abortive, 49; his kingcraft becomes mischievous, 50

Edward III., effects of wars of, 56.

Eighteenth century, the three great topics of the, 129.

Eliot, Sir John, his influence in the Commons, 107.

Elizabeth, Queen, a reconciler, because neither Romanist nor Protestant, 93; country and Commons justify this attitude, 94.

Emancipation, Roman Catholic, its result —disgusted Tories with their leaders, 194.

Empire, the, and the Popedom, 180.

Englishmen unideal, yet vanquished by an idea, 193.

Exclusiveness, the Roman aristocrat erred in, 10; ultimately engulfed in abyss opened by it, 11.

FEUDALISM weakened, 127.

Fox, Charles J., position of, 161.

"Fragments," the Plebeians not, 8, 9, 212.

Franciscans and Dominicans, the objects of the, 37.

Freeman and citizen interchangeable names, 7.

Freemen, the, admitted to Parliament because they could serve the country, 213.

GAUNT, John of, his sympathy with religious movement of Commons, 60; opposition of his descendants. 60.

George II., Frederick the Great contrasted with, 148.

George III., loyalty towards, 143.

German sovereigns, the, represent a principle, 143.

——— contradiction in reigns of first two, 144.

Gold, something higher than, must be represented, 64.

Grostête, Bishop of Lincoln, story of, 37.

HALLAM, Mr., why stood aloof from his party as to Reform Bill, 196.

Hampden's, John, influence in Commons, 107.

"Happiness, greatest, of greatest number" principle, 201.

Hare's, Mr., skilful and laborious scheme, 230; easy and simple in operation, 231.

Henry VIII., his want of sympathy with Commons, 69; his reformation insufficient, 70; claimed as natural head of reformers, 73; his relation to Parliament, 74; abuses in his time unite the Commons, 75; his character, 76; great instructor of his people, 76; his tendency to dogmatism, how checked, 77.

Hereford, Earl of. what we owe to the, 50.

Holy Alliance, the, a testimony to reality of Napoleon s dream, 177; its impotence, 178; inconsistency of sovereigns as to it, 178; combination of monarchs becomes the battle of nations, 174.

INTEREST, each, should have due expression and no more, 226.

JAMES I., the unfree king, 102; his Divine Right ideas drive Commons into antagonism, 103; his character, 103; his evil advisers, 138; the patron of bishops and literary men, 103; they oppose Commons as being puritan, 106.

James II., result of his career, 130; bishops and nonconformists alike compelled to change course, 131.

John's reign not beginning of English history —in what sense it may be so regarded, 43.

Johnson and Burke, what their intercourse proves, 149.

LABOUR, organisation of, its power, 205.

Lancastrian period, the, not progressive, 60.

Latimer, his relation to clergy and king, 78; his letter of appeal, 79; its object, 80; his warnings amid prosperity of Protestantism, 88; he and his friends held king representative of a higher, 91.

Leicester, the Earl of, his character, 35.

——— adheres to Robert of Lincoln, 39.

——— why earnest men sided with, 39.

Liberal idea, the, and nature s guidance, 170.

——— ideas after French Revolution, 168.

Liberty, Englishmen's notion of, 172.

INDEX.

Literature, English, born among struggles of the Commons, 54.
Literary class, the, its claims and possibilities, 228 : should not be a caste, 230.
Long Parliament, Cromwell consistent in dissolving the, 120.
Lords, the House of, a fit yet incomplete check, 227.
Louis Philippe's ambition, 179.
Lowe's, Mr., objections to further reform, 196; his arguments against it, 216, 217, 218, 220.

MACAULAY did little to recommend his own school, 132.
Majorities, United States an unfortunate instance as to, 224.
———— will of, not standard of truth, 201, 223.
———— working men no interest in exalting majority unto God's throne, 226
Manhood, to get greatest possible amount of, the chief problem, 211 ; it *must* be recognised, 212 ; by turning first to bodies the manhood will best be got at, 232.
Markmen, the, the great family unions, 17.
Mary's reign, test of citizenship in, 91.
———— contrasted yet connected with Elizabeth's, 92 ; Mary not a national sovereign, 92.
Material good insufficient, 180.
Mendicant friars, the, 51 ; centre of many influences, 53 ; the Commons, not nobles, oppose them, and why, 66.
"Merchant and Friar," the, 33 ; inferences from it, 45.
Milton, life and writings of, a clear comment on the time, 123 ; his belief that freedom belonged to man's spirit, 125 ; his great poem and New England, 126.
Mob, who flatters a, loves not a people, 201 ; danger of mere multitudes, 216 ; the effectual guarantee against mob-dictation, 232.
Money power, the, in the ascendant, 127.
———— no belief in Commons to oppose growing, 145.
———— Tory squires make some protests against, 146.
———— tendency to follow leaders possessing, 210.
———— or some other power ? 226.
Money standard on all hands confessed unsatisfactory, 221.
Moneyed class, the, kept other classes separated, 199.
Monopolies declared mischievous, 156.

NAPOLEON's ideal—republicanism wedded to monarchy, 171.
———— efforts, grounds for resisting, 173.

National life, result of the aspirations after 179.
Nonconformist suffering, the results of, 128.
———— influence, 158.
Norfolk, Earl of, what we owe to the, 50.
Norman ecclesiastics furthered assimilation of races, 28.

PARLIAMENT, why it thrust itself forward in Henry III.'s time, 41.
———— national element needed in, 227.
Parliamentary Reform impossible till rise of manufacturing power, 214.
Parties, providential restraints on Romanist and Protestant, 83.
Past, the, and future must be respected by legislation, 202.
People, the word often misunderstood, 2.
———— use of, in Shakespere's Roman plays, 3, 98.
———— why Macaulay uses "Commons" in place of, 3.
———— the Roman freeholder claimed title of, 4.
———— growth of, between reigns of James I. and Anne, 133.
———— sovereignty of the, what it means, 189.
———— full justice to the phrase, 201.
———— true servants of the, 202.
———— our history traces growth of, 206.
———— a, must be organic, 83 ; it must consist of freemen, 98.
"Piers Ploughman's Vision" indicates tendency of Commons, 54.
Pitt, the elder, a true instinct raised, 147 ; he spoke to a *heart* in the Commons, 147 ; of no Whig family, yet manifests Whig principles, 147 ; brings Crown into sympathy with Commons, 148.
———— the younger, his feelings about Reform, 151 ; he expresses characteristic feeling of 18th century, 152 ; objections to his scheme, 153 ; foreign questions supersede domestic ones, 154 ; Pitt's notion of Crown's discretion in withholding writs, 154 ; his prudence, 160 ; becomes cosmopolitan in view, 161.
Poorer classes, new provision needed for education of the, 184 ; how masses may best be packed together, 184 ; different courses proposed, 185.
Popedom, the, and the Empire, 180.
Poverty, terrible problem of, in Edward VI.'s time, 84 ; Latimer's views of it, 85 ; realm indebted for teaching to the sons of poor, not rich, men, 87 ; greed of proprietors, 87.

Press, the, valuable because representative, 62.
Protestants, great error of, 89; its result a reaction, 90.
Public affairs, apathy about, not safe, 219.
Puritan element, success of the, 113.
——— view of the king's trial, 119.
Pym, rise of civic feeling through, and others, 112.

RADICAL REFORMERS, the new class of, 190.
Reform, a minority for, in time of Henry VIII., 71; arguments of the opponents, 82; results of Reform, 84; general schemes of Reform inefficient, 223.
Reform Bill of 1831, its bearing, 195; old distinctions *nominally* preserved, 195; feelings of antiquarians as to it, 195; why Mr. Hallam stood aloof from his party regarding it, 196; it affirms, not contradicts, lessons of history, 196; admitting working men to franchise only unfolding its principles, 218.
Reformation, the, a protest for national order, 90; the peasants not satisfied with it, 95.
Reformers, the Protestant, expressed mind of nation, 72; what they urged on King Henry, 81.
Representatives, peoples', the Roman tribunes were, 9.
Restoration, the, what it brought back, 126.
Revolution, French, liberal ideas after the, 169.
——————— of 1848, how differed from the first, 199; difference not perceived by Chartists, 200.
Ridley and his friends hold the king to be a representative, 91.
Roman spirit, the, opposed to Christianity throughout, 13.
Romantic ideas dissipated by Bentham, 192.
Rousseau's lessons to the French, 170.
Royalist turncoats—Falkland and Hyde, 116.

SAVONAROLA, phenomenon of, his error, 68.
Saxon life, the, survived Norman Conquest, 26.
School, aim of, to fit men for citizens, 183.
Sect, rule of a, English will not bear the, 89.
Serfs or slaves, State bound to take care of, 99.
——————— could not be called Commons, 99.
Shakespere's historical plays, their great value, 99; the king his hero, this reverence derived from Elizabeth's position, 101; this justified by his Tudor experience, 137.

Slaves, the place of, in early British history, 18.
Sovereign, the, a fiction, 142; politicians may, a nation cannot, accept a fiction, 143; desirableness of limiting action of, 142.
Strafford in the way, 115.
Stuarts, followers of, had no distinctive principles, 108.
Suffrage, manhood, what it means, 207; contrasted with universal suffrage, 209; not a dream to desire all should be citizens, 209; manhood *must* be recognised, 212.
——— universal, what its adherents want, 210.
——— ——— effect of talk of, 211.
Supplies, right of granting, won *for* Commons *not* by them, 50.

TRADES, organisation of, how it exhibits freedom, 25.
Trades' unions, origin and attitude of, 214.
Tudor period, lessons of the, 96.
Tyler's, Wat, movement and what it meant, 57.

UNITED STATES, the, an unfortunate instance as to majorities, 224.
——————— prove that the people is not its own ruler, 225; Lincoln's words affirm true freedom, 225.
VOLUNTEER movement, the, its bearing on Reform, 221.

WALPOLE, Sir R., his management of the House, 145.
——— not a bad man, acted under a necessity, 145.
Watt and Arkwright, their influence on Reform, 155.
Wentworth, Thomas, policy of, 114.
Wesley and Whitefield, mission of, 158.
Whig and Tory in Charles II.'s time, 129.
Wilberforce, what his movement indicated, 166.
"Will of Majority," something more needed than, 222.
Winchelsey, Archbishop, what we owe to, 50.
Wordsworth on Man, 164; his sonnets on Liberty show process of reaction, 172, 175.
Working men, no interest in exalting majority unto God's throne, 226; difficult questions made easy by admission of working representatives, 233; mainly impulses may be derived from that, 234; their faith in right, 234.
Wyckliffe opposes mendicant friars, 53.
——— Wyckliffites, the, become Lollards, 61.
——— put down by Lancastrian princes, 67.

THE WORKING MEN'S COLLEGE,

FOUNDED 1854.

45, GREAT ORMOND STREET, BLOOMSBURY, W.C.

Principal—REV. F. D. MAURICE, M.A.

Council of Teachers.

R. BARWELL, Esq., F.R.C.S.
T. R. BENNETT, Esq. M.A., Christ Church, Oxford.
T. BODLEY, Esq., M.A., Cambridge.
Rev. J. S. BREWER, M.A., Queen's College, Oxford.
Mr. BROCK, C.S.
Rev. W. J. BRODRIBB, M.A., Fellow of St. John's College, Cambridge.
Mr. J. BUNNEY, Landscape Painter.
ARTHUR COHEN, Esq., Magdalen College, Cambridge.
Rev. J. Ll. DAVIES, M.A., Trinity College, Cambridge.
LOWES DICKINSON, Esq., Painter.
E. S. FORD, Esq., M.A., Oxford.
F. J. FURNIVALL, Esq., M.A., Trinity Hall, Cambridge.
Mr. GRUGEON, Certificated Teacher of Botany (Science and Art Department of Privy Council).
J. W. HALES, Esq., B.A., Fellow of Christ's College, Cambridge.
Rev. S. C. HANSARD, M.A., University College, Oxford.
THOMAS HUGHES, Esq., M.P., B.A., Oriel College, Oxford.
Mr. W. JEFFREY.
D. C. LATHBURY, Esq., M.A., Brasenose College, Oxford.
J. LEE, Esq.
*R. B. LITCHFIELD, Esq., B.A., Trinity College, Cambridge (*Treasurer*).
J. M. LUDLOW, Esq., Lincoln's Inn.
GODFREY LUSHINGTON, Esq., M.A., late Fellow of All Souls, Oxford.
VERNON LUSHINGTON, Esq., B.C.L., Trinity College, Cambridge.
JOHN MARTINEAU, Esq., B.A., Trinity Hall, Cambridge.

* These Members of Council form the Executive Committee.

THE WORKING MEN'S COLLEGE.

N. S. MASKELYNE, Esq., M.A., Wadham College, Oxford.
A. J. MUNBY, Esq., M.A., Trinity College, Cambridge.
ALEXANDER MUNRO, Esq., Sculptor.
EUG. OSWALD, Esq., Professor of French.
J. Y. PATERSON, Esq., B.A.
W. P. PATTISON, Esq., Actuary.
G. J. PEARSE, Esq., M.A.. Trinity College, Cambridge.
F. C. PENROSE, Esq., M.A., Magdalen College, Cambridge.
VAL. C. PRINSEP, Esq.
*Mr. HENRY RAWLINS.
Mr. JOHN ROEBUCK, C.S., Fellow of the College.
DANTE G. ROSSETTI, Esq., Painter.
Mr. W. ROSSITER, C.S., Fellow of the College.
JOHN RUSKIN, Esq., M.A., Christ Church, Oxford.
J. R. SEELEY, Esq., M.A., Fellow of Christ's College, Cambridge, Professor of Latin in University College.
J. SLADE, Esq.
A. SONNENSCHEIN, Esq.
Mr. W. T. SUTTON, C.S.
*Mr. GEORGE TANSLEY, C.S., Fellow of the College.
W. CAVE THOMAS, Esq.
Mr. W. WARD, Drawing Master.
J. WESTLAKE, Esq., M.A., late Fellow of Trinity College, Cambridge.
Mr. S. WILKINS.
THOMAS WOOLNER, Esq., Sculptor.

Fellows of the College.

Mr. WILLIAM ROSSITER, Mr. J. ROEBUCK, Mr. G. TANSLEY.

Associate.

Mr. D. LEGATT, LL.B.

OBJECTS OF THE COLLEGE.

The College was founded in 1854. The students are, for the most part, working men; and the teachers are, in general, members of the Universities and of different professions, or those who have themselves been students in the College. Its purpose is to unite these classes together, by associating them in the common work of teaching and learning. It provides instruction at the smallest possible cost (the teaching being almost wholly unpaid) in the subjects with which it most concerns English citizens to be acquainted, and thus tries to place a liberal education within the reach of working men.

THE WORKING MEN'S COLLEGE.

CONSTITUTION OF THE COLLEGE.

The College is divided into six Classes :—
(1.) The general body of MATRICULATED STUDENTS.
(2.) CERTIFICATED STUDENTS, that is, those to whom at the end of any course shall be awarded a Certificate of Competency in the subject of the course.
(3.) SCHOLARS, that is, those who prove themselves competent in any one department of the College studies.
(4.) ASSOCIATES or permanent members of the College, being such students as have shown by examination that they have attained the degree of liberal education which the Council believes to be within the reach of members of a Working Men's College.
(5.) FELLOWS: These will be chosen out of the Associates. The Fellows will take part in the education of this College, and may assist in establishing and carrying on other Colleges. They will be chosen by the Council, after due consideration of what they have done in the Associate Examination, and of what they have been since they entered the College. Moral qualities, a capacity for teaching, and a willingness to teach, will be at least as indispensable as proficiency in any study.
(6.) The COUNCIL of TEACHERS: it is intended that the Council be recruited from the Fellows, to the extent of at least a third of its members. The Council will be prepared to assist in the formation of new Colleges, in London or other parts of England.

GENERAL SYLLABUS OF COLLEGE STUDIES.

⁎ *For details see Special Syllabus of each Department.*

MATHEMATICS.

1st Year.—*Preparatory:* Arithmetic; Preparatory Geometry and Mensuration; Book-keeping.
2nd Year.—*Pure Mathematics*, Geometry (*Euclid, Books* 1 *to* 4); Algebra, to Quadratic Equations.
3rd Year.—*Pure Mathematics:* Geometry and Conic Sections; Algebra and Trigonometry.
4th Year.—*Applied Mathematics:* Statics; Dynamics; Hydrostatics; Optics.

Fee, 3s. *each Term.*

LANGUAGE AND LITERATURE.

ENGLISH:—1st Year.—Parts of Speech: Etymology, Analysis of Sentences.
2nd Year.—Advanced Grammar: History of the English Language.
3rd Year.—Literature.

FRENCH:—1st Year.—Elementary Grammar: *Accidence, Syntax, Etymology.*
2nd and 3rd Years.—Literature.

GERMAN:—1st Year.—Grammar.
2nd Year.—Literature.

LATIN:—1st Year.—Grammar.
2nd and 3rd Years.—Literature.

GREEK:—1st Year.—Grammar.
2nd and 3rd Years.—Literature.

Fees, one hour a Week, 2s. *each Term.*
„ *two hours a Week,* 3s. „

PHYSICAL SCIENCE.

The Subjects taught in this Department are:—

Natural Philosophy.
Botany.
Physiology.
Zoology.
Physical Geography and Geology.
Chemistry.

No order strictly definable. (See Special Syllabus.)

Fees, one hour a Week, 2s. *each Term.*
„ *two hours a Week,* 3s.

HISTORY, INCLUDING GEOGRAPHY.

1st Year. { *Preparatory English:* two terms.
{ *General English:* two terms.

2nd Year. { *Constitutional History of England:* two terms.
{ *General History of Europe:* two terms.

General Lectures on Literary and Social History, Ancient and Modern History.

Fees, one hour a Week, 2s. *each Term.*
„ *two hours a Week,* 3s. „

Bible Class Free to all Members.

The subject of *Bible History* is considered in a separate set of lessons, which are delivered on Sunday evenings, and are free to all Members.

DRAWING.

Elementary—Light and Shade.
      From Casts of Natural Objects.
      From Leaves, Birds, &c.
      Colour—Studies from Still Life.
      Drawing from the Antique.
      Drawing from the Life, without colour.
      Painting from the Life.
         Fees, 4s. *each Term.*

MUSIC.

SINGING CLASSES. THREE SECTIONS, viz.:
  III.—Learning to read by the Scale, and from the "Tonic Sol-fa' notation.
  II.—Part Singing, Choruses, Glees, &c. (common notation.)
  I.—Advanced Part Singing; music of Handel, Mozart, Mendelssohn, the Madrigal writers, &c.

    Fees: SECTION I., 1s. 6d. *the half-year.*
       „ SECTIONS II. and III., 2s. „

ADULT SCHOOL.

JUNIOR SECTION.—Easy Reading, Writing, and Arithmetic.
SENIOR SECTION.—Reading, Writing from Dictation, Practical Arithmetic, Rudiments of General Knowledge.

    Fee, 6d. *a week.*

GENERAL LECTURES.

General Lectures on the College Studies are given every Saturday at 8.30 P.M. During the first term of each College year these lectures are by the teacher upon the special work of their respective classes.

EXAMINATION REGULATIONS.

The Examinations are held in the last week of December. Examinations for Certificates are also held at the end of each course of study.

Candidates for a Certificate must have attended the College for at least four terms, and for a Scholarship or an Associateship at least eight terms.

CERTIFICATES.—Every class is examined at the end of its course, and Certificates are adjudged to those students who show a competent know-

THE WORKING MEN'S COLLEGE.

ledge of the subject. The names of those who, though not obtaining Certificates, pass the Examination with credit, are posted on the walls of the College. Every member of the class is expected to submit himself for this Examination.

ASSOCIATESHIP.—To become Associates, Students must pass an examination in the following subjects, viz. :—

(1.) Bible History; (2.) English History; (3.) English Grammar; (4.) Arithmetic up to Fractions and Proportion.

They must also either obtain, or have obtained Certificates in any two of the following subjects, viz. : Algebra and Advanced Arithmetic; Geometry; Conic Sections; Botany; Physiology; Geology and Physical Geography; Mechanics; Hydrostatics; Optics: English History, with questions in General Geography; English Language; Logic; Music; Drawing; French; Latin; German; Greek. (If Mathematical Subjects only are taken, however, *three* certificates will be required.)

SCHOLARSHIP.—Candidates for a Scholarship in any Department will be examined in the subjects specified under the corresponding head in the following list :—

ART.—

HISTORY.—General knowledge of English History; a particular knowledge of either Constitutional, Literary, or Social History of England; Outlines of Ancient History or of Modern History.

LANGUAGES.—English, (including Grammar;) French or German; Elements of Latin.

MATHEMATICS.—Algebra; Geometry; Trigonometry; Mechanics; Conic Sections; Astronomy.

PHYSICAL SCIENCE.—Natural Philosophy; Botany; Physiology; Zoology; Geology; Chemistry. Any three of these subjects.

For further details as to Examinations, inquire of the Secretary at the College.

The COLLEGE YEAR begins about the end of October, and consists of four regular Terms of eight weeks each, and a Vacation Term of from eight to ten weeks. A Programme of Studies for each term is printed before its commencement.

The LIBRARY is open to students every day (except Sunday) from 7 till 10 P.M. Books can be borrowed for the Vacation.

The COFFEE and CONVERSATION-ROOM adjoin the Library, and is open from 7 till 10.30 P.M. Tea, Coffee, &c., is provided at reasonable prices.

A CONVERSAZIONE is held in January and in July of each year. A Benefit Society has been formed in connexion with the College. Strangers are admitted. Tickets 1s. each.

The COLLEGE RIFLE CORPS (consisting only of Members of the College) forms the first three Companies of the 19th Middlesex, which

THE WORKING MEN'S COLLEGE.

is commanded by Lieut.-Col. THOS. HUGHES. The subscription is four shillings per year, to efficient members, which covers the cost of Membership of the College; to non-efficient members, fourteen shillings. Subscriptions may be paid quarterly or otherwise. Applications should be made to Captain MARTINEAU, BAILEY, or FURNIVALL, at the College.

GIRLS' SCHOOL.

A School for Girls under fourteen years of age is taught by Ladies at 45, Great Ormond Street, every day of the week, except SATURDAY and SUNDAY.—Charge 6d. per week, for Girls under ten; 9d. a week for Girls under fourteen years of age. Hours, 10 to 1, and from 2 to 3.

PLAN OF COLLEGE STUDIES.

The plan of study which the Council desire the students to follow may be best gathered from the scheme of the examination for Associateship. The intention of that examination, and of the examination for Certificates of Competency, is to give coherence and method to the class-work of the College, by keeping within the view of both teachers and students a plan of study variable according to diversities of circumstances and tastes, but representing, as well as a formal scheme can, the kind and degree of "liberal education" which the Council believe to be within the reach of the students of a Working Men's College.

The peculiar circumstances under which the work of such a College is carried on forbid any attempt to require all students to follow certain prescribed courses of reading, as has hitherto been done in other Colleges. The choice of subjects of study is therefore left to each student's discretion; but the Council are anxious to impress upon those whom they have to teach the necessity of attending to the following recommendations, which they give as the result of several years' actual experience. They would earnestly advise the students—

(1.) Not to join any class unless they have a reasonable prospect of being able to attend regularly, and *to find time for study out of the class*. Without this last condition, it is nearly impossible that they can make any good use of the class teaching.
(2.) To consider before they undertake any subject the amount of work it will probably involve, as compared with the amount of leisure they have to devote to it.
(3.) To inform themselves on these and other points by consulting the detailed syllabus of studies, and by personal inquiry of the Teachers.

To assist in making the work of the classes as systematic as possible, the following Rules and arrangements are adopted:—

THE WORKING MEN'S COLLEGE.

(1.) Admission to any class is given only by the teacher of the class.

(2.) On the first class night of every course the teacher will explain the subject and method of study, answer inquiries of intending students, and ascertain if students desiring to enter the class are sufficiently advanced to do so with advantage.

(3.) Practice classes are attached to the regular classes; and it is expected that students will attend these as part of the regular College work.

(4.) A class may be suspended at the option of the teacher when the number of students attending it falls below six.

(5.) Students should, if possible, join their class the first night; but it is left to the teacher's discretion to admit them later.

ADMISSION OF STUDENTS.

Students must be above sixteen years of age. They must be able to read and write, or must go to the Adult School in the College to qualify themselves for the College Classes.

Students can join the College at any time, but the regular time of entering the Classes is the beginning of the College year—about the end of October. In some subjects elementary classes are also formed at the beginning of the third term—early in March.

At entrance, each student pays a Fee of 1s. 6d.: also a Term Fee c. 1s. for every Term he attends the College. Each class is entered and paid for separately.

November, 1865.

WORKING MEN'S COLLEGE BUILDING FUND.

STATEMENT BY THE COUNCIL.

45, Great Ormond Street,
December, 1865.

"This College was founded in 1854. The students are, for the most part, working men; and the teachers are, in general, members of the Universities and of different professions, or those who have themselves been students in the College. Its purpose was and is to unite these classes together, by associating them in the common work of teaching and learning. It provides instruction at the smallest possible cost (the teaching being almost wholly unpaid) in the subjects with which it most concerns English citizens to be acquainted, and thus tries to place a liberal education within the reach of working men."*

In carrying out these objects, we have had some measure of success. The number of students was, at the end of the first term, 145; it is now 509. In the year 1857, finding the hired house in which we had begun our work too small, we purchased, for £1500, the large freehold house and ground which we now occupy. This was effected by means of a loan of £1000, and a gift of the remaining £500 from the Principal. The debt so created has since been reduced to £400 by savings from the current income, aided by the unsolicited donations of friends. With the increase in the number of students has come an increase in the number of classes and subdivisions of classes; and for some time past we have been sorely pressed for space. This pressure has been and is a serious hindrance to the progress of the work of the College—a hindrance daily and hourly felt. Further removal being for many reasons out of the question, we have no option but to *build*.

We want chiefly these things—

(1.) A room or rooms for the Art Department, the rooms now occupied by the Drawing Classes being entirely unfit for the special purposes of an Art School. [No department of our College has been more successful than our Art Classes, carried on from the first under the general supervision of Mr Ruskin. We may say that at no period of the

* The "General Prospectus," from which this paragraph is extracted, and the Programme of Classes for the current term, will show in detail the nature of the work done in the College.

existence of the College have we ever had space enough to admit all who would have wished to join these classes.]

(2.) A moderate-sized hall or room for General Meetings, Lectures, and social purposes, capable of containing some 300 or 400 persons. [Such meetings have now to be held in the "drawing-rooms" of our present house, to the great inconvenience and discomfort of all who take part in them.]

(3.) A better room or rooms than we have now got for the Adult School. [The School serves at once as a feeder to the College and as a field for the exercise in tuition of our students, by whom exclusively it has always been carried on. It has an average attendance of about 35 per week, and is now held in a kitchen and back kitchen.]

(4.) A room to contain a Museum, and serve as a Natural History class-room. [We have considerable geological and other collections, chiefly accumulated by the members of the Physical Science Classes; but for lack of space they cannot be properly arranged or effectively used. The only room which can now be spared for a "museum" is one not much larger than a closet, and the Physical Science Department of the College is from this cause debarred the possibility of progress or expansion.]

(5) More small rooms for classes and general purposes. [We not only have a difficulty in accommodating the classes, but have also to make the Library serve as a Secretary's Office, and have no room available during the class hours for committees or other business.]

The site of the proposed building is already provided. The freehold ground on which the College stands runs about 160 feet back in the rear of the house. The College also owns (subject to a mortgage) the freehold of the adjoining house and a similar plot of garden in its rear; the two together form a quadrangular plot 18,000 square feet in area, of which a space containing 12,000 square feet is now available as a building site.*

The Building, we consider, should comprise on the ground floor the required Hall, separable into divisions for the purposes of the Adult School, and above this a room or rooms specially adapted for the Studio of the Art Department. One or two small rooms may be added as funds allow on the ground floor with the possibility of continuing the buildings along the sides of the quadrangular space at some future day, if necessary. The space set free in our present building by the removal of the Art Department and the Adult School will provide the required "Museum" and class-room accommodation.

* This adjoining property we acquired six years ago (with a view to securing space for such an extension as is now desired) by purchase, applying thereto a sum of money which two friends of the College placed at our disposal for a time. The house, with a part of the ground behind it, is now let on a lease for 21 years, at a rent which exceeds by £64 the annual interest of its mortgage debt. We have thus a sinking fund by which, in 17 years, that debt will be extinguished.

THE WORKING MEN'S COLLEGE.

We are advised that such a building as this can be well and substantially built in a plain but good style for about £3,000 to £3,500. A cheaper building might possibly answer the end immediately in view, but we are anxious that whatever is put upon the ground shall be not unworthy of the purpose which it is to serve. The College will, we hope, outlast the present generation, and we must therefore make our buildings worthy to range with any others which our successors may erect when the present houses are taken down.

As a proof that the College has taken root in a congenial soil, and has borne ripe fruit already, we need only refer to the fact that by this time it has trained a large proportion of its own teachers. Of the thirty-two whose names figure on our programme for the first term of the twelfth year (1865-6), no less than twelve are Fellows and certificated or other students of the College; they carry on, for instance, the whole of the Mathematical teaching of the first year's course, and take part in that of the second. We are thus, in an educational point of view, to a great extent self-supporting.

Financially we are so likewise. For several years, thanks to the excellent administration of our funds by a Students' Finance Committee, the income from Students' fees has met our current expenditure, leaving a margin available for the reduction of our mortgage debt. But the sum now wanted would fall heavily on a few contributors, such as those friends who from time to time have kindly assisted us with donations or subscriptions. We have never yet asked money of the general public—we think we are justified in doing so now.

Considering the vast endowments which the benefactions of former ages have provided for the education of the people, endowments to which the wealthiest of us are the most indebted, it would be a disgrace to a wealthy metropolis like this if it were necessary to beg long at the present day for the inconsiderable sum we are now asking for. We should be sorry to say that our College is as good as it might be made, or even that is as good as we might have made it. But we can say honestly that it is doing, and has been doing for eleven years past genuine work. Its present need goes far to testify to this. And the amount of labour and thought which is being voluntarily devoted to the undertaking, and by none more freely than by our students, affords, we think, some guarantee that we shall not mispend what may be given us. Finally, though many a single purse might well defray our needs, we may perhaps especially commend them to those who would be willing to take part in the teaching of this and other Colleges if they were not prevented by professional and other avocations. Will they not share our work by helping us to develop it?

Signed, on behalf of the Council of Teachers,

F. D. MAURICE, *Principal.*

THE WORKING MEN'S COLLEGE.

Contributions may be sent to the LONDON AND COUNTY BANK, Oxford Street Branch, ("Working Men's College Account,") to the SECRETARY, at the College, (P. O. Orders to be payable to Thomas Shorter,) or by cheques payable to the order of the Treasurer, R. B. LITCHFIELD, Esq., 4 Hare Court, Temple, or to any member of the Council of Teachers.

The following donations have already been received or promised:

	£	s.	d.		£	s.	d.
His Royal Highness the Prince of Wales	26	5	0	Mrs. F. J. Furnivall	2	2	0
Rev. F. D. Maurice, Principal, from publication of Lectures on the Suffrage	100	0	0	*Mr. W. Jeffrey	5	0	0
				C. D., per Rev. F. D. Maurice	50	0	0
				*W. P. Pattison, Esq.	10	0	0
Ditto (proceeds of delivery of the same Lectures at the College)	12	7	10	The Duke of Argyll	5	0	0
				Mr. Sergeant Manning	5	0	0
				John Vincent, Esq.	5	0	0
Conrad Wilkinson, Esq.	52	10	0	Richard H. Hutton, Esq.	2	0	0
John Stuart Mill, Esq., M.P.	5	0	0	*Thomas Woolmer, Esq.	2	0	0
				Henry Footman, Esq.	5	0	0
*Vernon Lushington, Esq.	50	0	0	Shadworth H. Hodson, Esq.	25	0	0
Samuel Morley, Esq., M.P.	21	0	0	Vincent S. Sean, Esq.	5	0	0
A Friend, per Rev. F. D. Maurice	10	10	0	Somerset Beaumont, Esq., M.P.	10	0	0
*Arthur Cohen, Esq.	10	0	0	Sir T. Fowell Buxton, Bart., M.P.	30	0	0
W. Powell, Esq.	10	0	0				
Sir Charles Bunbury	5	0	0	*Mr. John Roebuck, New York (certificated Student, and Fellow of the Working Men's College)	10	0	0
Francis Turner Palgrave, Esq.	5	0	0				
Andrew Johnston, Esq.	5	0	0				
Hensleigh Wedgwood, Esq.	5	0	0	*Godfrey Lushington, Esq.	20	0	0
Sir Thomas Phillips	5	5	0	Sir John Lubbock, Bart.	5	0	0
Miss Caroline Fox	1	1	0	Andrew Johnston, Esq., (2nd donation)	20	0	0
*J. Lee, Esq.	1	1	0				
G. Dornbusch, Esq.	1	1	0	"Heavy Dragoon"	3	0	0
George Godwin, Esq., F.R.S.	1	1	0	Alexander Macmillan, Esq.	10	10	0
Rev. Henry Sandford	1	0	0	C. B. Locock, Esq.	15	0	0
Frank Crisp, Esq.	0	10	0	Miss Irby	3	0	0
*The Rev. J. Ll. Davies	10	0	0	Miss Swanwick	5	0	0
*D. C. Lathbury, Esq.	5	5	0	Howard W. Elphinstone, Esq., M.P.	5	0	0
*R. B. Litchfield, Esq.	25	0	0				
*John Westlake, Esq.	20	0	0	Miss E. R. Allport	1	0	0

* Members of the Council of Teachers.